THE DANISH
FOLK
HIGH SCHOOLS

Denmark's International
Study Program

DANISH INFORMATION HANDBOOKS

THE DANISH
FOLK
HIGH SCHOOLS

Second revised edition
by
THOMAS RØRDAM

DET DANSKE SELSKAB

Copenhagen
1980

Translation:
Alison Borch-Johansen

Printing:
AiO Tryk as, Odense

Acknowledgement:
For lending illustrations, the author and the Danish Institute express their
gratitude to the Folk High School Information Office and to the Folk High
Schools involved.

*The Danish Institute for Information about Denmark
and Cultural Cooperation with other Nations*

Kultorvet 2, DK-1175 Copenhagen K.
Tel. (45–1) 13 54 48

ISBN 87–7429–028–2

Printed in Denmark

Contents

I.

HISTORICAL BACKGROUND

Seats of Culture

Denmark is a small country: a sixth of the area of Great Britain with just over five million inhabitants. It is unusual for a nation of this size to arouse the interest of other countries. But there are three things for which Denmark is well known abroad. First, Hans Andersen's stories; second, social welfare; and third, the Folk High Schools.

These schools are a special feature of Danish culture. They have left their mark on public life, home life, the schools, and the Church. Through its ideas, inspiration and practical work, the High School movement has strengthened Danish democracy, based on the principle of freedom of thought, religion and speech (in the words of the High Schools' founder, N. F. S. Grundtvig, »to think, believe and speak freely«). With the establishment of the High Schools, Denmark became the pioneer country in free popular education[1] in Scandinavia as a whole,

---

1. The expression »free popular education« does not carry quite the same shade of meaning as »adult education«. The word »free« signifies not only that the students join the course voluntarily, but also that there are no examinations of any kind. Basically, the aim of this kind of education is determined by the individual – not by any public authority or public opinion. The words »popular education« refer to the great popular movements of the 19th century and to *Grundtvig's* use of the word »oplysning«. It is almost synonymous with the English word »enlightenment«, but the Danish word is suggestive of something more than mere knowledge. Grundtvig makes »livsoplysning«, i.e. enlightenment on the life of man, the crux of his ideas (*Vide* the chapter on Grundtvig's »Ideas for a Folk High School«). *Enlightenment on the life of man* is the key word for the understanding of what the Danish Folk High Schools want to give their pupils.

although in our sister nations High Schools have developed along the lines of their individual national and cultural patterns. The Danish Folk High Schools are Denmark's most important contribution to the educational debate throughout the world. Since they reflect the changes in our social structure, and social progress, they too are subject to the laws of evolution. This has brought new gains, some experiments have been rejected, but their purpose and basic principle remain unchanged: enlightenment on life.

The High Schools became seats of culture in Danish society. Some foreigners even identify the Folk High Schools with all examination-free Danish educational activity. However, this is not correct. The High Schools have had to hold their position *vis-à-vis* a number of competing educational initiatives. Nevertheless, the ideas behind Grundtvig's High Schools have given inspiration to other types of schools. Their influence has spread to the rest of society like rings on the water. Seen in the historical perspective, the Grundtvig Folk High Schools started a stream which has spread out into a delta, in which its outlets are Continuation Schools, Free Schools, Evening High Schools, Agricultural Schools, Domestic Science Schools, Pensioners' High Schools, etc., etc. In addition, in the course of nearly 150 years, High Schools have been established representing very varied attitudes to life – popular, religious and political[1].

1. Several Folk High Schools and Grundtvig Free Schools were founded in connexion with the Free Church circles which emerged in the wake of the popular religious revivalist movements in the first decades of the 19th century. The »Valgmenighed« (Elective Congregation) Act of 15 May 1868 permitted a group of residents in one or more parishes to start an Elective Congregation, the members of which could elect and pay their own pastor. The latter, however, is subject to the same Established Church Authorities as the parish clergy appointed by those authorities. The Grundtvig Free Congregations are closely related to the Elective Congregations, but unlike them, do not belong to the Established Church. The members' choice of a pastor does not need to be approved by the Minister of Ecclesiastical Affairs, as the Free Congregations do not come under the Church Authorities. He cannot, therefore, issue legal certificates of church ceremonies. Danish Free Congregations were also established in South Jutland whilst it was under the Germans from 1864 to 1920.

The High Schools did not come into being as the result of any official initiative. They came from the Danish people themselves. Later popular educational activities were started on the initiative of the State and of Local Authorities. But the Grundtvig Folk High School has left its stamp upon them.

The Danish national character is reflected in the Folk High Schools, because the core of the Danish nation – earlier the country people, but in this century also townsfolk – took part in their formation. The democratic way of life runs like a gold thread through the whole history of the High Schools, established as they were at a time in the last century when representative government had replaced the Absolute Monarchy. They placed themselves at the service of the Parliamentary Government.

A Static Peasant Society

In the society in which Grundtvig (1783–1872) grew up, the Danish peasants were a poor, unfree, despised social class. In their deep degradation, in the middle of the eighteenth century, the tenant farmers were subject to villeinage and bound to the soil and the locality. During the 1780's, however, the situation began to improve, when close co-operation between the Absolute Monarch, prominent Civil Servants and humane land-owners led to agrarian reforms. Adscription was abolished. From now on, peasants could move freely wherever they wished. Common tillage came to an end. The tenant farms gradually became free-hold. The farms were moved out on to what had been common land, outside the old closed villages. And yet it would be many years before the typical Danish landscape, with its scattered farms and small-holdings, took shape.

The men, whose efforts had led to this work of reform, wished it to be followed up with educational reforms. But in influential circles, the predominant view was that an increase in knowledge would make the peasant and his class intransigeant. In 1799, however, bold and occasionally somewhat unrealistic educational reformers did establish an agricultural school on Falster. But no pupils presented themselves. The peasants were conservative, and wished to follow in their fathers' footsteps. In spite of the agrarian reforms, Denmark remained a static peasant society.

In the census of 1801, three-quarters of the population lived in purely country districts. And it was poor. In 1813, the State went bankrupt. After 1818 came the great agricultural crisis. The town societies of the time were not only small, they were also far fewer than today. Copenhagen, with 101,000 inhabitants, was roughly the size of all the other towns put together.

Town and country were two sharply divided worlds. Intellectuals in the towns had nothing but contempt for the peasants. This infected the rest of the townsfolk, for whom the country population was simply a vast grey mass. There were considerable class differences everywhere. The children of each class were supposed to remain in the class in which they had grown up. It is true that there were no legal rules to prevent a son from seeking a different employment from that of his father. But society was so static that this was rare. There was therefore no noticeable drift to the towns.

There was no public opinion on how society should be arranged. The common people – peasants, small-holders, country craftsmen and servants – lived on in accordance with tradition, without indulging in speculations as to how matters could be improved. People bowed to the authority of the land-owners and public officials, and they had implicit faith in the King, and in his absolute sovereignty.

Continuation Schools and Higher Peasant Schools

Decades were to pass after the economic agrarian reforms, before it was realised that some elementary knowledge of arithmetic and writing was indispensable. In 1814 came the great school reform, with which compulsory education was introduced – although not compulsory school attendance – for all children between seven and fourteen. Here at last was the break-through for the spirit of enlightenment of the eighteenth century, and the desire to give ordinary people better education. This was expressed most strongly in the Education Act, § 28, which obliged teachers to hold evening classes for young people over Confirmation age twice a week. The purpose of this provision was not only for young people to have the opportunity of brushing up what they had learned in primary school. They were also to be familiarized with »the duties which their more mature age and changed conditions carry with them«.

This statute presaged a new epoch. In the 1820's the first attempts were made to hold evening classes. In the case of one of the first Folk High Schools (Uldum High School) the establishment of the school can be traced back to this work with evening classes.

However, it was the revolutions in various European countries which really gave impetus to the efforts for popular education. The reverberations of the July Revolution in Paris in 1830 also reached Denmark. In 1831, the Advisory Councils were established in the provinces, and the peasants received seats, although their eligibility was limited. This was the first step towards a constitutional change which introduced representative government. Now the voice of the peasants was to be heard in public matters. And this was not all. In the years 1837–41 Local Councils were set up, bringing fresh justification for the demand for education.

There was no question of a real political awakening. But even though the peasants still evinced little interest in their rights of political freedom, they understood the necessity for the land reforms to be carried further. They realised that if their social conditions were to be improved, better education was needed than that given in the primary schools, for – as one of the peasant leaders of the century put it – »knowledge is power, ignorance is slavery«. Nor was it enough to have evening classes in a few village schools. As late as 1848, only 9% of them held evening classes, and those were mostly for the sons of farmers, following their Confirmation.

As part of these educational efforts, the farmers themselves took the initiative in establishing continuation schools. In this connexion, the demand also arose for *higher peasant schools*. When the Constituent Assembly had assumed office in 1848, some

11

plans were proposed for the State to set up farmers' schools, one in each county, intended for the most intelligent and brightest sons of farmers. This aim was not achieved however. The higher peasant schools which were established were only for local pupils. They were strongly influenced by the educational ideas of the eighteenth century, and by the religious revivalist movements at the turn of the century, and not so much by Grundtvig's ideas for high schools, although even then he had already put them forward in written form.

Grundtvig's ideas for high schools constituted a new departure, but there is considerable evidence that even without Grundtvig, we should have had schools for young adults from the farming community. They would have been technical agricultural schools, or schools for general education with final examinations, and they would mostly have been day schools meant for young people in the locality. But under the influence of the Folk High School men, who were inspired by Grundtvig, popular education was raised to a higher level.

II.

GRUNDTVIG'S CONCEPT OF ENLIGHTENMENT

Priest, Poet and Pioneer in Folk Education

Grundtvig's portrait hangs on the walls of many of the century-old village halls in Denmark. And deservedly. The popular cultural and topical political lectures which have been held throughout the years in these halls are a legacy from Grundtvig. They have been an important factor in the religious and cultural movement which received the designation »Grundtvigianism«. He worked untiringly throughout his life, as clergyman, poet and folk educator. His hymns are sung in church every Sunday. Every year, when the bells of Copenhagen Town Hall have rung the New Year in, the Radio Choir joins in with »Welcome, year of the Lord«. At weddings, the climax is »It is so lovely to walk together«; at funerals, »Church bells never to cities«; and when we wish to be solemn and patriotic, »Mother's name is a heavenly sound«. All of them Grundtvig's. But first of all he is a Christmas poet. 22% of the songs in the High School Song Book are his. In all, he wrote 1600 hymns and songs. The Grundtvig historian Kaj Thaning has calculated that his collected works would fill 130 large volumes.

Nikolaj Severin Frederik Grundtvig was born in 1783 and died in his ninetieth year. He still influences the debate, with his views on Church and school. Only a small part of what he wrote has been translated, whereas Søren Kierkegaard's works have been translated into many languages. This has nothing to do with their respective importance in Denmark, however.

Grundtvig is very difficult to translate. Insight into his world of ideas is necessary, as well as familiarity with Nordic ancient history. His style is peculiarly Danish, although the complicated syntax of his sentences shows a thorough knowledge of Latin. In addition, the most ordinary words are given special meanings, and the countless words he created demand a considerable work of interpretation.

Grundtvig's interest in educational questions must be seen on the background of his personal experiences, during childhood and adolescence. He was born in Udby Vicarage, but was sent at the age of nine to the Vicar of Thyregod, where he was taught at home. In Grundtvig's opinion, this was the ideal form of school, as it retained the atmosphere of home. At the age of fifteen he was sent to a »Latin« (grammar) school in Århus. This he considered a sojourn in the wilderness. He came to hate the »black school« and »bookworm culture«. In 1854 he wrote, »if there was a question of abolishing all the grammar schools in the country, I would vote for it«. They were »spirit-consuming, stupidity-producing institutions«, where the boys were alienated from real life. In a pamphlet from 1834, *The Danish Fourleaf Clover*, he stated that »the only good boys schools I can think of are clever and energetic citizens' houses, where boys both acquire a taste for the activities they will later pursue, and get a grip on them . . .«

»A simple life, a merry heart«

Grundtvig gives expression to his views on people and education in a poem from 1839, »An open letter to my children«, of which the following three verses are an excerpt. It is set to music. These three verses have often been sung in the High Schools:

> Give me a simple life, a merry heart,
> And kings may keep their pomp and garments splendid;
> Let me in hut or mansion live the part
> Of one from worthy ancestors descended,
> With eye for things above as God ordained,
> Awake to greatness, goodness, truth, and beauty,
> Yet knowing well the yearnings unattained,
> Thro' knowledge, great achievement, deeds, and duty.

A wholesome life like this have I desired
To be my children's aim and aspiration;
And when my soul was from its brooding tired,
My childhood prayer brought me consolation;
Then from the Spirit came this truth to me:
That God's own garden full of joy is growing
On earth, when we will give ourselves to be
The plants of Him from whom all life is flowing.

But we may not expect the ripened fruit
Except through growth, the law of all creation;
In spring we see the green and tender shoot;
In early summer like a revelation,
A burst of glory, flowers bright unfold;
Then through the sunny summer days appearing
The fruit matures for harvest: So the soul
Is only step by step its harvest nearing.

(transl. S. D. Rodholm)

In this poem Grundtvig draws a parallel between human life and the seasons of the year. As childhood corresponds with the spring, youth is compared with summer, maturity with harvest, and old age with winter. As an opponent of »boy scholarship« he gives a warning against forcing a child's development. The child is like a plant. Only when the child has been able to grow unhindered in the spring, can he blossom in the summer, later to bear fruit. The character of maturity must not be pressed into the child's mind.

Pestalozzi and Rousseau also declared that the most important purpose of the school was not to stuff knowledge into a child's mind, but to develop human nature, making the child and youth receptive to life, and bringing him into concrete relationship with its practical activities. Grundtvig was undoubtedly influenced by these teachers, but he did not share Rousseau's naturalistic view of man.

Sorø School

Grundtvig's ideas for Folk High Schools were linked with the problems surrounding the budding democracy during the last years of the Absolute Monarchy. In the 1830's, when his most important writings on the High School concept were published, the first steps towards democracy had been taken, as mentioned above, with the establishment of the Provincial Advisory Councils. At this stage Grundtvig was profoundly anxious for the future. He was afraid of »a minority of skilful, clever men exploiting certain forms of government«, afraid of the grammar schools poisoning the boys, who would later become the leading men in government, and afraid of a revolutionary rising, if democracy was not established on a broad cultural foundation. It was a question of life or death for the whole Danish nation, whether or no the High School he visualized being set up in Sorø Academy, as a State initiative, came into being.

At this »school for everyday Danish life and citizenship«, »general education, far beyond religion, writing and arithmetic«, was to be provided. It was to be a school for »folk character«, which in Grundtvig's usage did not mean »loved by the people«, nor »popular«. He was not thinking of popular education. He meant »likeness to the people«, that is, Danish in mentality, as far as language and traits, tradition and common destiny allowed. He went in for a human education, not implying »humanitarian« in the sense of »good-natured« or »philanthropic«, but an education based on people's own premises, their history and poetry. He was opposed to the idea that a people's education should be decided by men so distant in time and place as the Romans and the Greeks, or by Latin or Greek.

The High School was to be a »school for life« in contrast to the grammar school, which was a »school for death«. It was to give an »awakening« enlightenment. But here he was not thinking of anything exalted or religious. He was not thinking of the religious Revivalist preachers. By »awakening« or »life enlightenment« Grundtvig visualized: bringing out the life which one could presume was already present in everyone. He found an interpretation of the basic conditions of human life in the Nordic myths. They reflected »the spirit of the people«. The school for life was to be »historical poetic«, but the poetry was not to be understood as aesthetic. It had nothing to do with the poet whose introspection is occupied with ephemeral moods and

Ludvig Schrøder (1836–1914), the founder of Askov High School and its first principal, at the rostrum, surrounded by teachers and pupils. On the right, the composer Heinrich Nutzhorn, (standing) Jacob Appel – Schrøder's successor – the physicist Poul la Cour and the student of folk life H.F. Feilberg. Painted by Erik Henningsen 1902.

J.Th. Arnfred (1882–1977), the third principal of Askov, lecturing.

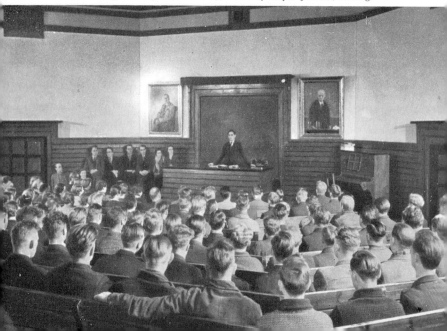

Ernst Trier (1837–93) during one of his lectures at Vallekilde High School, which he founded, and of which he was principal for nearly 30 years (1865–93).

Peter Manniche (born 1889) the founder of the International High School, and up to 1954 its principal, leading a study circle at his High School, where he not only had international students but also introduced new teaching methods.

external forms. The path led to those who had seen visions with poetic clarity, and had been able to interpret them, so that they had illuminated human life.

Romanticism had opened Grundtvig's eyes to Nordic mythology. In 1802, he was influenced for life by the lectures on German Romanticism given by his cousin, the philosopher Henrik Steffens, at Copenhagen University. They convinced him that the invisible world, the world of the spirit, was the real world, and that »the living word« through which the spirit was expressed, possessed creative power. Life enlightenment should therefore be provided primarily through conversation. Men were different from other living creatures in that they could speak. But unlike some of his imitators among later Grundtvigian High School men, he considered that there could be something domineering and didactic in the lecture form. In conversation, »a lively interplay« could arise between teachers and pupils, and between the pupils themselves, without any planned result being arranged deliberately by the teacher. An important pre-condition was the comradeship between teachers and pupils in daily life at a High School, corresponding to what he had himself shared during a period of study at Trinity College, Cambridge.

Modern Grundtvig Research

Kaj Thaning has shown that the political situation before the advent of the Folk High School was only the external reason for Grundtvig's writings on his ideas for High Schools. There was also an inner cause: deep personal experience in connexion with his visits to England around 1830, which brought about a change in his view of the relationship between Christianity and human life.

He had previously held the view that life on earth was a testing period, a pilgrimage to the true life after death, which meant that life on earth was reduced to something sinful. But now he realised that human life had its own significance. It was »a divine experiment in dust and spirit«, and this divinely created human life was not to be transformed according to cer-

Christen Kold (1816–70)

tain Christian norms. Now he wished to take life as it was. Christianity was not a law, but a gospel, which should give life a new form. In his High School writings he never used the word »education«. »Man is not a monkey«, which has to be trained. So he spoke of enlightenment. Now he differentiated more clearly between human and Christian enlightenment. He secularized his view of the High School. At the school for life, »*natural* life should be strengthened and grappled with«, as he wrote in 1837 in a pamphlet entitled »To Norwegians on a Norwegian High School«. Now he was an advocate on behalf of life and human nature. He said: »First the man, then the Christian.« This should not be understood, however, in the sense that Christianity is the result of human development. He also said: »We receive Christianity for nothing, it is pure joy.« But this did not prevent the High School from giving enlightenment on Christianity, when occasion arose.

The decisive point was that Grundtvig now engaged in polemics against his own earlier belief, that Christianity was a condition for all things human and national. From now on he joined forces with non-Christians, in so far as they committed themselves to this life, and regarded it as something more than »biology and other uninspired worship of knowledge«. He wished to co-operate with them, if they were »people with spirit«, and if they regarded life as a struggle. This was the kind of explanation of life that he received from his heathen Nordic forefathers, and not from the exact sciences.

When Grundtvig spoke of life enlightenment, it was therefore neither as a Christian nor as a theologian. He spoke deliberately within the framework of human life on this plane. His bugbear was academic education. Without genuine Danish common sense we should be lost in abstract internationalism. But within this framework people should be free to think, believe and learn whatever they wished.

To the end he opposed those who had doubts as to freedom at school and in the Church. But he rejected the French Revolution's individualistic concept of freedom. He applauded the Nordic concept, where freedom was based on an obligation towards human society.

The Fate of Sorø School

Sorø School was originally intended for the coming members of the Advisory Councils. Later, Grundtvig thought of expanding the school to include young people from all classes, »tenants and free-holders, both great and small, craftsmen of all kinds, sailors and business men«. For it was not »likeness to the people« for farmers and academic civil servants to live in two quite separate worlds. The school must build a bridge across this gulf. And since it was to be for the whole population, the school must be »without any payment for knowledge« and without entrance tests or final examinations.

Here all the great and small problems of the day could be discussed »in friendly fellowship«, when interest and thirst for knowledge were present. The school was not to help its pupils to earn money or build careers, but to help »everyone to return to their jobs with added zest and with greater insight into their living conditions as men and citizens«.

In a paper written in 1840 Grundtvig visualized Sorø School being governed in »the King's and the people's spirit«, with the Advisory Councils of the time as its model. There was to be a School Council corresponding to the Advisory Councils. Although the principal of the High School would have authority to decide whatever he wished, in all important questions he would be expected to hear the opinions of the school council, the members of which would practically all be elected by the pupils. In this way, they would gain a better insight into the government of the country, and be prepared to take up their duties as members of the Advisory Councils.

Grundtvig was less interested in the choice of syllabus. He attached particular importance to the subjects Danish and history. The latter was to be taught as »the moving life history of the human race«. He saw a parallel between the course of history and the individual's life. From history one could gain experience for use in life in the present and future. He emphasized that a human being is only something in the historical context into which he is born, and which one cannot run away from, without the individual's or the people's life degenerating into isolated fragments – incomprehensible and meaningless.

Christian VIII was favourably disposed towards Grundtvig and his plan to turn Sorø Academy into a Folk High School. He ordered the university and grammar school authorities to submit a recommendation on the matter. These were in no hurry, however, and Grundtvig was not given a seat on the commission which prepared the education plan. The basic provisions on the conversion of Sorø Academy were confirmed by a Royal Resolution of 31 December 1848. However, the King died soon after, and two months later, the Absolute Monarchy was abolished, with the introduction of the new Constitution. Professor J. N. Madvig, who became Minister of Ecclesiastical Affairs and Public Instruction, and who was himself a stiff classicist, shelved the idea for the Sorø School. He did not want a »separate educational institution, monopolising the character of Danish patriotism«.

With this, Grundtvig's plan to reform education from above was nullified. At about the same time, however, an opportunity appeared for a reform from beneath. Higher peasant schools were established in the country districts. Instead of a State High School at Sorø, many small schools were started on private initiative, inspired by Grundtvig, but stamped by the educator Christen Kold.

The Plan for Göteborg and the Marielyst School

Grundtvig's ideas on education had a wider perspective than the Sorø school. The crowning glory was to be a joint university for the whole of the North in Göteborg (Gothenburg, Sweden). This Nordic School of Graduates depended upon each of the Nordic countries first having their own High Schools and their own teachers colleges for training the staff.

He developed this idea in 1839 in his High School pamphlet *On the Scientific Union of the North*. The Göteborg university was to be a place of work for Nordic scholars. 300 professors, humanistic and scientific, would here be able to devote themselves to research, free from any examination system and in lively interchange »for the happiness and advantage of the human race«. They should collect young people around them in free studies, with »orderly, scholarly conversation«. This was more important than writing books or reading them. But it should not be anything in the way of a folk university or a folk academy for popularized science. On the contrary, he criticized the existing Nordic universities because they did not concentrate sufficiently on pure scientific research. The special training for the Civil Services should be carried out in special schools or colleges.

Such a university, collecting young people from all over Scandinavia in college life, as in Cambridge, cultivating conversation like the old Greeks, would be able to break down national prejudices and unite the Nordic peoples. The three Nordic peoples' differences in language and nature should not be apparent, because, in spite of all the differences, they had »the Nordic spirit« in common. The existing universities in Copenhagen, Christiania (now Oslo), Uppsala and Lund, which were stamped with classical Latin education, could then be closed down.

Grundtvig's plan for a common Nordic university was not realised, any more than the Sorø School, but indirectly it became the inspiration to the start of the *Folk Academy of the North* in 1968.

In 1856, *Grundtvig's High School at Marielyst* was founded, however, with a fund which friends in Denmark and Norway had collected for Grundtvig's birthday in 1853. The dedication read in part: »The money shall be used for a Folk High School, to be organised in accordance with your decisions and bear your name, and be a modest beginning of the building which you have had in mind.« The clergyman and hymn-writer C. J. Brandt was appointed the first principal of the school. Part of Grundtvig's opening speech was as follows:

»I saw life, real human life, as it is lived in this world, and saw at once that to be enlightened to live a useful and enjoyable human life, most people did not need books at all, but only a genuinely kind heart, sound common sense, a kind good ear, a kind good mouth, and then liveliness to talk with really enlightened people, who would be able to arouse their interest and show them how human life appears, when the light shines upon it.«

21

Grundtvig was not, as many in Germany believe, the »prototype of the once so highly prized and later – rightly – rejected marriage between national self-glorification and Christianity«, declares Professor Götz Harbsmeier in his thesis »Who is the Man?«[1] He argues against the Germans who have claimed that in this eulogizer of Danish nationalism one can recognize some of the ideas which National Socialism went in for. This can be due to the difficulty in translating the Danish word *folkelighed* (likeness to the people). In Grundtvig's usage, *folkelighed* has no nationalistic smear. Harbsmeier points out aptly, »The wicked part of National Socialism and Neo-Nazism and Fascism is the misuse of what a people, its history, its language and its culture really mean.« »But«, he continues, »because love of country, fellow countrymen and language have been so wickedly misused, nevertheless, love of country is not identical with nationalism or Nazism.«

The view of Grundtvig as a somewhat provincial Danish nationalist stems also from ignorance of the connexion with the universal in which the idea of *the national* appears in his High School writings. He turned against the humanism which looks at humans unconnected with place and time, and fails to take people's national – i.e. natural and historical – background into consideration. For this reason he combatted Renaissance culture. It was brought to Denmark from outside, in foreign dead languages, Latin and Greek, and built upon cultural values to which the people had no access. It was reserved for the elite, not for the people. It created a gulf between the people and the elite.

The interplay between people, mother country and Christianity was closer in the Grundtvig High School circles than with Grundtvig himself. But even with this reservation, it has been stated with truth that after the war with Bismark, which led to the loss of Southern Jutland in 1864, the Grundtvig Folk High Schools became bastions of the Danish way of life – bastions of a different and more lasting kind than the Viking Dannevirke wall

1. Vandenhoeck und Ruprecht, Göttingen 1972.

across South Jutland, or the site of national tragedy at Dybbøl. They became fortresses for defence in the Danish struggle for existence against the German great power. Harbsmeier writes:

»This enforced defensive Danish 'nationalism' has nevertheless contained a criticism of national self-glorification and any tendency to make the national factor all-important. In addition it contained a loathing of dictatorship, propaganda, terror and racialism. But because of language difficulties, if for no other reason, this will be difficult for German readers to understand.

»We Germans have given the Danes a critical attitude towards the perversion of nationalism, once and for all. It is therefore easy to understand that this defensive nationalism withdrew into the background, in the Danish Folk High Schools in 1950–70. The 'High School nationalism' which has constantly been fed by the feeling of oppression from the south ever since Grundtvig's time, has had to yield.«

Grundtvig's national feeling (which is not the same as nationalism!) was inevitably nourished by the necessity for creating a shield against the looming military monster in the south, and had its roots in an irresistible attraction towards the people's heathen past. But for him it was not a question of creating a new human type, as it was for the National Socialist movement. His aim with the Folk High School was not to be his people's sculptor. But he was often misunderstood in this respect, in the High School circles influenced by late Romanticism. From this arose the infatuation for him in National Socialist circles in the Hitler period. The fact that in Denmark, too, it was believed that his ideas for the High Schools were only a national Danish matter, has been a great hindrance for a right understanding of him. In reality, his High School ideas were so comprehensive and timeless that it has been possible to make them bear fruit in quite different social conditions from those in which he himself lived.

III.

THE HIGH SCHOOLS BEFORE 1864

Was the High School Concept originally German?

After the introduction of the Advisory Provincial Councils in the 1830's, the idea of starting higher peasant schools also arose in Holstein, the German province in the Danish monarchy. Led by the monastery syndic Karl Friedrich Hermann Klenze (1795–1878), from Uetersen near Hamburg, a circle of peasants from the Rendsburg district published an open letter to the Advisory Councils in Slesvig and Holstein demanding »a higher folk school« for young people after Confirmation. It was to be »a nursery garden for clever chairmen of local councils and deputies to the Advisory Councils«. Klenze wanted »an institution for the nurture of political and economic areas of interest«. He advocated the establishment of such a school on the grounds that the majority of the Advisory Council Deputies in Slesvig and Holstein ought to be peasants, since peasants formed such a large proportion of the population. Such a school was needed »for the support and reinforcement of the State, and in the course of 10–15 years, the peasants would be able to send independently-minded deputies with an all-round education to the Advisory Councils«. In German-speaking Holstein, the primary schools did not provide teaching in anything but reading, writing and arithmetic, any more than did those elsewhere in the monarchy. The man in the street must also have a share in higher education. But Klenze may very likely not have known of Grundtvig's High Schools.

In 1842, the Rendsburg Higher Folk School was able to open

on a German basis. There was no national aim in this. The school wished to have Christian VIII as its Protector. Julius Heinrich Lütgens was appointed principal. Whilst Klenze attached most importance to civic education, Lütgens aimed at letting cultural and business education go hand in hand. Pupils over the age of 20 received, for example, lessons in scripture and philosophy, local and world history, German and social science. The courses were originally for two years, but later had to be limited to one year.

The school aimed particularly at helping young people who were thinking of leaving agriculture. Hence the social science. But it did not last long. In 1849 it was closed after the collapse of the Slesvig-Holstein revolt.

A former principal of Rendsburg School, Dr. Fritz Laack, has put forward the opinion that the oldest Folk High School in Denmark, at Rødding, which was started in 1844 in the Danish-speaking North Slesvig, was inspired by Rendsburg School and organised on the same lines. But this is not correct. Rendsburg School was a rural equivalent to the secondary schools of the towns. It was an examination school, and it was only a day school. Rødding was a Folk High School. It was an examination-free school, and from 1845 the pupils had their full board and lodging at the school. It was not established as a parallel to Rendsburg School, which was »patriotic, not Slesvig-Holsteinian«, but as a bulwark against the Germanization of the Danish-speaking North Slesvig. It was in Rødding that the type of school developed which later, somewhat altered under the influence of Christen Kold and others, became, not only in Denmark but also abroad, what is understood by the designation Folk High School.

Rødding High School's First Years

The background for the foundation of Rødding High School was the struggle over nationality in South Jutland. The conflict flared up at the beginning of the 1840's. In 1844 it was laid down by royal decree that German was to be the official language in the Slesvig Advisory Council. Only those who were not able to speak German were allowed to speak Danish. It caused a sensation, therefore, when the German-speaking but Danish-minded Haderslev merchant, Peter Hjorth Lorenzen, took the liberty of speaking Danish in the Advisory Council. He was the first man to understand the importance of a Danish school for young people, for even in the wholly Danish-speaking North Slesvig, all advanced teaching was carried out in German. German was the courts, church and school language in four Danish market towns and fifty Danish parishes. But the real motive force behind the start of a Danish school for young people in this province was Christian Flor, who was professor of Danish literature at Kiel University. He was strongly influenced by Grundtvig's ideas on enlightenment, and on 4 July 1944, Grundtvig was one of the principal speakers at a folk meeting on the historic Skamlings Hill. With the support of a national liberal aid society in Copenhagen, Flor succeeded in obtaining an interest-free loan for the purchase of a farm in the village of Rødding. And this was turned into a High School.

On 7 November 1844, the first pupils arrived at Rødding High School. They came in jolting horse carts, with clothes cupboards on the tail boards. There were only 22 pupils, of whom 20 were from South Jutland. The first principal of the school, Johan Wegener, and his staff faced a difficult task. In those days the peasants were suspicious of everything new and untried, and these peasants were to be guineapigs, and in a type of school which had never been tried before.

The pupils were put up in farms in the village. But this was not a happy choice. The temptation to smoke, drink and play cards was too strong. A house for the pupils was therefore arranged for, the following year, to house 30 pupils.

At the opening of Rødding High School, Wegener made an inaugural speech which was certainly above the heads of the pupils. But on the other hand it is interesting for posterity. In words which are surprisingly topical to the debate of our time, on the object of the Folk High School, he said in part:

»We will found a school, a Folk High School for the farmer and the citizen. The purpose of this school, just as of other schools, is to teach, form and refine youth.

But it is established with special consideration for the farming class; and here such knowledge and skills will be learned as are especially useful to this class. No one is to be educated here for coming positions, nor given knowledge through which he can obtain a particular career in the Civil Service. It is presumed that the young men who are sent to this institution will be and remain farmers and citizens, and we shall simply try to teach them what is necessary for them to be able to function as independent, courageous men in society . . .«

It was a »school for life« and not for social advancement that this High School pioneer had in mind, even at this early stage, and although all the pupils were farmers' sons, the school deserved the name of Folk High School. It aimed higher than did the higher peasant schools which were started in the years which followed.

Wegener emphasized that patriotism in its best sense did not include nationalistic xenophobia:

»To love one's country is not to hate one's enemy, and still less to shut one's eyes to the very beautiful and good to be found in other nations. The German folk are a great and grand folk, and Scandinavia's nearest blood relations. Kinship, neighbourhood, culture and outlook, common interests, the same sufferings and fears, the same hopes and desires, to some extent also the same virtues and faults should make these folk our best friends.«

Wegener brought great expectations to the High School work, but was disappointed. The pupils, who were from 16 to 27 years old, were far more raw and ignorant than he had imagined. At Christmas 1844 he decided to seek a parson's incumbency at the close of the winter term. But by the time he was to leave, he had changed his opinion of them. In a letter to his fiancée he writes:

»The greatest possible attention reigns, they devour every word, and are eager to get everything written down. This was more than I had believed possible. They are wildly ignorant, and yet their spirit is so good that many of them understand the most delicate nuances and hints.«

Christian Flor

Wegener was succeeded by Christian Flor, who gave up a Chair at Kiel University, to move to Rødding. He was responsible for the day-to-day management of the school from 1845–47. In the winter 1845/46, the school already had 42 pupils. The original idea had been that the school term should be 1 1/2 years, but because of the work in the fields, it was impossible to get the pupils to remain at the school during the six summer months.

In his annual report on Rødding High School for 1846 Flor wrote:

»Final examinations we do not have. The most important part of our teaching at the High School is not the positive proficiencies and skills that we seek to give the pupils, but rather the spiritual life which is awakened and nurtured in them, so that their understanding becomes sharper, their judgement more mature, their hearts more open and nobler, that a sense of order and beauty and a zestful life is aroused in them, and that desire for occupation can take the place of the usual habit of apathy, and their feeling of comradeship and patriotism become more permanently nourished and strengthened. It is impossible for all this to be displayed in a public examination.«

The weekly timetable was divided as follows: Danish history: 3 hours. Geography: 3 hours. Comprehension exercises (moral, psychological and statistical subjects): 4 hours. Danish: 6 hours. German: 3 hours. World history: 3 hours. Natural history: 2 hours. Drawing: 4 hours. Arithmetic: 2 hours. Geometry: 2 hours. Gymnastics: 4 hours. Singing: 2 hours. In all: 38 hours. The hours of lessons were from 8–12 in the morning and from 2–5 in the afternoon. From then until the evening meal at 8 p.m. the pupils did their preparation for the lessons the following day. In addition they took part in amateur theatricals, a school newspaper, etc.

There was no hearing of pupils in the intellectual subjects. The six hours a week devoted to Danish made this the most important subject. Often the teachers read from a poetical work and commented on it. But the idea was, before all else, that the poetical work should be experienced. Analytical treatment took second place. The line of demarcation between literature and Danish history was not sharply drawn. It is a matter of opinion, whether the teaching which the first High School men imparted on the basis of historical poetic subjects should be called Danish literature or Danish history.

For Flor, who had lectured to students at the university, his work at the High School must have been a strange experience. The peasants who sat on the student benches had had to drive cattle to pasture, as boys, and much of the time they had been quite alone. This lonely life and their responsibility for the animals gave them a stamp of seriousness which is unknown among our young people today. There was little opportunity for amusement. Many of them had only been away from their home parishes while they were in »the King's uniform«. But all this made them receptive to the »enlightenment for life« in historical poetic context.

The social conventions between the pupils had a certain formal tone, although with a tendency to democracy. Flor's plan – in harmony with Grundtvig's ideas – was to let the school teachers and pupils together form an educational council, with far-reaching powers, but this was strongly opposed by members of the School Board of Directors. The pupils' council's sphere of action was limited to the maintenance of general discipline and good tone at the school.

Sofus Høgsbro

During the Slesvig-Holstein revolt in 1849–50 – also called the 3 years war – Rødding High School had to close. It was re-opened in the winter 1850/51, its principal being Sofus Høgsbro, later well known as a Liberal politician. In the meantime, the democratic Constitution of 1849 had been introduced in Denmark. When Høgsbro presented his programme for the school, he applauded the newly won freedom, but stressed at the same time the responsibility which was bound up with freedom. Rødding High School must give enlightenment on folk citizenship. The pupils should be given a helping hand to understand their own times. His teaching therefore laid particular weight on modern history and social conditions. Never before had Grundtvig's thoughts on enlightenment for citizenship been more fully realised than at Rødding High School in Høgsbro's time. This was the nearest approach to Sorø School, although on a simpler level than Grundtvig had visualized. Grundtvig was also elected as Deputy for the school.

Høgsbro's ideas for the High School work were given in his annual report on Rødding High School for 1858:

»The High School must not produce blind fanatics, but enlightened conscientious citizens. It must give the pupils as faithful a picture as possible of actual conditions, it must make them aware of the different opinions there are, emphasizing the most important reasons that are put forward for and against, try to awake a sense of the various questions and interest in their solution, and by developing their abilities, both of head and heart, give them the possibility for this. But it should not give them the solution. This they must give themselves. It is only thus that their spiritual life becomes their possession, it is only thus that they will later be able to enter civil life, as independent, thinking people.«

A High School man from our times could hardly have formulated the general educative and civic educational outlook more clearly. But not all the teachers shared his views. Even in Flor's time, there had been some trouble about the school, as an agricultural teacher, who was highly respected, thought that the school should attach greater importance to agricultural technical teaching and natural science. History and poetry should play a lesser role.

In Høgsbro's time, the old conflict flared up again. In the Slesvig Society, which owned the school, there was a body of opinion advocating the conversion of the school into an agricultural college. Now that the war was over, with the defeat of the Slesvig-Holstein rebels, their national task had been completed. But the proposal met opposition for widely different reasons. No less than three groups, each of them led by teachers at the school, had their private plans for Rødding High School. In opposition to Høgsbro, the agricultural teacher Edv. Thomsen wanted an agricultural college. Another teacher, Jens Knudsen (the poet Jakob Knudsen's father), wished on the contrary that the school should find its ideal in Christen Kold's viewpoint, and lay much greater weight upon revival to national and Christian life. In the end, however, Flor succeeded in bridging the differences.

The school enjoyed the favour of the State, in the form of considerable subventions, and it was always well supplied with educational ideas. Now it was not so much a South Jutland frontier school as it had been previously. After 1850 there were

30

even classes of pupils where the South Jutlanders were in the minority. And the pupils who came from other parts of the country were not so interested in national political frontier questions.

In 1862 Høgsbro left the school to enter political life. He was replaced by Ludvig Schrøder, who was principal up to 1864, when the school had to close in consequence of the loss of South Jutland. Under him, Rødding High School received a more Christian character. Under the German regime, it was turned into a girls school, which was retained until 1885.

In the period 1844–64, Rødding High School was attended by 522 pupils in all. But in general, they did not only belong to the peasant class. In that period, support was not given to pupils from needy homes. An investigation shows that of the 267 pupils who came from South Jutland, 176 were from well-to-do farmers' homes, and 25 from large country properties. There were few sons of small-holders. There was even more social imbalance, tending upwards, among the pupils who came from the rest of Denmark. Among them there were also a number who came from culturally interested Grundtvigian clergy homes.

Rasmus Sørensen and Uldum

Whilst Rødding High School was founded on an academic initiative, there were other High Schools, which were started before 1864, as the result of the farmers' own efforts for enlightenment. These were technical agricultural schools, and were marked by the educational ideas of the eighteenth century. Among the moving spirits behind this work the principal figure was the peasant agitator, Rasmus Sørensen from Venslev on Zealand, who was familiar with Grundtvig's High School plans. He had taken the teachers' examination – characteristically enough from a college which owed its foundation to the agricultural reformer Chr. Reventlow – and started a High School in the village of Uldum near Vejle. Unlike the university men at Rødding, he felt himself to be one of the peasants' own men. His work sprang from the conflict with the clergy, who were the peasants' and the village teachers' superiors.

A clear line runs through Rasmus Sørensen from the religious revivalist movements, which swept through the country in the first years of the nineteenth century, and up to the democratic political life which appeared with the Constitution of 1849. In his speeches and writings, he demanded that the laws of the agrarian reform be carried further. But the essential condition for this was that the State could no longer keep the peasants in ignorance. They should not wait for the State to build schools for them. They should themselves see to it that higher peasant schools were built, to vindicate the interests of their class. Rasmus Sørensen approached the High School cause on the basis of demand and need. He knew the currents of thought among the common people, whilst Grundtvig was a prophet and seer. Rasmus Sørensen understood that the High School ideas took root most easily, where a religious revival had prepared the ground in advance. He therefore chose Uldum. There had been a pietist lay movement here, and here he had many friends. A large room was hired from one of the farmers in the place as a school room, and in 1848 the school could open its doors. But his teaching career, like Wegener's, lasted only a short time. As a result of the war against the Slesvig-Holsteiners in 1848–50, he had to give up after a few months. He did not achieve much of importance, therefore, as a practical working High School man. It was with his almost apostolic folk revivalist efforts that he won his reputation and was important to the High Schools thereafter.

In 1851, Uldum High School re-opened in a new building, paid for by friends of the school. Rasmus Sørensen had appointed another village schoolmaster as his successor, E. M. Rotwitt. According to Rotwitt's teaching plan, the oral Danish lessons were not only to be concentrated on »book reading both of prose and poetic contents«, but also on »reading newspapers and other publications«. He aimed at complying to a greater extent than Rødding High School with the farmers' and the pupils' own wish to include the reading of agricultural publications in his Danish classes. This was later also customary at other higher peasant schools. This was useful if the farmers were to make their voices heard on equal terms with »the educated

Holger Begtrup (1859–1937). His historical works, and more than 5000 lectures throughout the country made him one of the leading figures in the High School world.

Hjalmar Gammelgaard (1880–1956) did more than any other man to make Danish workers aware of the High School ideas.

J.Th. Arnfred (1883–1977) the personification of Danish democracy, was for decades the permanent link between the Folk High Schools and the Co-operative Movement.

Johannes Novrup (1904–60) was the internationally-minded philosopher and humanist of the Folk High Schools.

Map of Danish Folk High Schools in the year 1877 made for this book by professor Roar Skovmand.

Danish Folk High Schools affiliated to the Folk High School Information Office by 1 January 1980.

■ General Folk High Schools
○ Gymnastics and Physical Training High Schools
▲ Pensioners High Schools
● Youth High Schools

Knud Rasmussen ○
GREENLAND

Nordiska Folkhögskolan ■

■ Vrå

■ St. Restrup
■ Støvring

■ Krabbesholm ■ Pinsevækkelsens
■ Nørre Nissum ■ Den lille
▲ Den jyske Pensionist
○ Gym. i Viborg
■ Nørgårds
■ Holstebro ■ Hadsten ■ Rønde
Egå ● ■ Sproghøjskolen på Kalø
■ Vestjyllands ■ Silkeborg ○ Idræts. i Århus
■ Herning ■ Ry ● Unge Hjem
■ Familiehøjskolen ■ Testrup ▲ Kolt
■ Vestbirk ■ Odder ■ Ask
■ Uldum ■ Elbæk ▲ Rude Strand
■ Odder ■ Egmont
SWEDEN
■ LO-skolen
■ Den internationale
■ Krogerup
■ Grundtvigs ■ Luthersk Missions
■ Brandbjerg ○ Den jyske Idræts ■ Vallekilde ■ Tidens
■ Engelsholm ■ Kunsthøjskolen ■ Borups
■ Børkop ■ Ubberup ■ Roskilde
■ Snoghøj ■ Bâring ■ Tølløse
■ Esbjerg ■ Kolding ■ Brogården ○ Søhus
■ Askov ■ Internat. Apostolsk
■ Rødding ■ Andebølle ■ Den danske Husflids
● Ungdomsh. ved Ribe ■ Assens ○ Gerlev ■ Haslev udvidede
■ Forskningshøjskolen ○ Køng ■ Skælskør ■ Haslev
■ Hoptrup ■ Ryslinge
■ Løgumkloster ○ Gym. i Ollerup
Kvindeh. ■ Uge ○ Den røde ■ Europahøjskolen
■ Rønshoved ■ Danebod ■ Rødkilde
○ Idræts. i Sønderborg
■ Jaruplund Ærø ■ Lollands Bornholm ■

High Schools not attached to the Information Office and therefore not included in the map: The Travelling High School (Tvind, Juelsminde, and Vamdrup), the Nursing Sisters' High School (Højbjerg), Marielyst Pensioners High School (Væggerløse) and the Workers' High School (Julianehåb, Greenland).

Knud Rasmussen's High School, Holsteinsborg, Greenland.

Askov High School. The building on the left, with half-timbered gable, houses the school hall. The building on the right contains the music room and the belfry.

people« *vis-à-vis* the authorities. Examinations were also held. But these took the form almost of lectures.

Rotwitt also acknowledged his debt to the religious revivalist movements after 1800. When a proposal was put forward in Parliament for religious freedom, a number of the Danish clergy collected addresses to the Government and Parliament for the rejection of the proposal, because in their opinion it would encourage the sectarian movements. But Rotwitt was among those who courageously opposed this, and warned the public against the clergy's requests for signatures. Such disobedience against a civil servant had Rasmus Sørensen's full sympathy. Grundtvig later succeeded in carving a pathway between the religious assemblies and the Established Church, when he entered the contest for a law on the free choice of a pastor, and the abolition of the exclusive right to preach of the parish priest, and for the Voluntary Elective Congregations Act.

Apart from this, Uldum High School led a quiet life. No remarkable High School programme speeches were made as at Rødding, but Uldum soon became the centre for large popular meetings.

In 1861, Rotwitt was elected to Parliament, and his connexions with the school were loosened.

Other Peasant High Schools

In Rasmus Sørensen's home district west of Næstved, in an area with good Zealand soil and large estates, the peasant agitator, Peder Hansen, Lundby, wanted a school for farmers' and small-holders' grown-up sons. The conditions were good. There had been a considerable stir among the country people, since the 1830's. Religious revivalists and later the »peasants' friends« had a solid foothold in this part of Zealand, and in 1852, Hindholm High School was started by the Head of Holsteinsminde children's home, Anders Stephansen. Hindholm was situated quite close to the children's home. It was not a political, one-sided high school, even though its connexion with the »peasants' friends« was maintained all through the 1850's.

Peder Hansen particularly wished to have small-holders' sons at the school, but the majority of the pupils were sons from solid farmers' homes. Hindholm became simply the High School for the Zealand farmer class.

Like Uldum, Hindholm was not especially Grundtvigian in its aims, but both Anders Stephansen and his successor, Chr. Nielsen, attached great importance to the pupils feeling themselves as links in the nation's solidarity. Nielsen regarded it as the duty of the High School to inform the young people of »as great a part of the experience and knowledge that at the present stage of development are older educated people's common knowledge . . . in fact arouse spiritual life in our youth«.

Hindholm had an excellent teaching staff, and became a large school, the only Danish Folk High School before 1864 to have over 100 pupils during the winter semester. History was the principal subject. Weight was laid particularly upon Danish history, which was taught in free lectures. In addition, Danish geography and statistics were taught, as well as law. Danish was also a central subject in the school syllabus. Scripture was not taught, but the school had a certain Christian character. Examinations were not held, and the pupils were to be grown-up, preferably from the age of 18 to 26. It was sometimes difficult, however, to get the farmers to understand that such a high minimum age could be necessary.

Staby Peasant High School near Ringkøbing, which was founded in 1852, was a continuation school for the locality. The youngest of the pupils was not yet 14, and the great majority were under 18. Amongst the subjects taught were Danish composition, Danish history, geography, botany, soil study and mathematics. This was one of the higher peasant schools where examinations were held. This was also the case at *Lars Bjørnbak's High School* at Viby near Århus, started in 1857. Bjørnbak was strongly influenced by Rasmus Sørensen. These purely informative higher peasant schools and continuation schools, started before 1864, were regarded by some Grundtvigian High School men as secondary schools, because they held examinations, and therefore as suspect institutions. They were not successful in the long run. They succeeded best where the principals, like the brothers Lars and Thomas Bjørnbak (the latter established a school in Vend-syssel), were also political folk revivalists.

A far more important influence for the future was the example of the educator Christen Kold.

A Socrates in Peasant Clothing

No one has done more to give the Danish Folk High School the plain, homely character which is still typical of it than Christen Kold (1816–1870). What Rasmus Sørensen did not attain, although he aimed so high, Kold achieved. He had the persever-ance and obstinacy which Rasmus Sørensen lacked. His speech was also for simple souls. Conversations with this Christian Socrates in homespun peasant coat were an inexhaustible source of inspiration to his pupils throughout their lives.

Kold was the son of a cobbler in Thisted. Like Rasmus Søren-sen, he was the product of the religious revivalist movement originating among the Moravian Brethren. He was greatly in-fluenced by his mother and all that she had told him as a child, and by Søren Kierkegaard's »Deeds of Love«. He had read this book as a young man.

Kold went to a teachers college. Here he passed through several spiritual crises. But then he had the opportunity of hearing the Grundvigian peasant and lay preacher, Peder Lar-sen Skræppenborg, who drove around Jutland in his own horse-cart, and sang and spoke with his childlike piety and tremend-ous vitality. Previously, Kold had thought of God as a severe chief of police, always ready to punish. But Peder Larsen's mes-sage, that God loves mankind, made him exclaim: »I have never known anything like the life, the joy, the strength and energy which rose up in me.« He told everyone he met of this: »Have you heard that God loves mankind, also you and me?« People shook their heads, and thought he had gone mad. But it made no impression on him. In his exalted enthusiasm he walked barefoot from the college to Thisted, to follow in the footsteps of the Disciples. Boys threw stones after him, and made fun of the strange man.

As a new-fledged college graduate he became a tutor in the

home of a rich farmer in South Jutland. Among the children there was a little girl who was unable to learn her lessons by heart. Kold noticed that when he related the contents of a book, little Maren could repeat it word for word the following day. He realised that he could awaken the children's interest in the Bible stories and Danish history far better by telling them, instead of following the usual practice, with the children learning by heart and then being heard. Rousing story-teller as he was, he made the children want to go on studying the material on their own, and gave them food for their imagination and emotional life. With his stories he shifted the centre of gravity from external things to the children's inner reality. One day, when Kold had been telling his class the first part of the story about Abraham's sacrifice of Isaac, one boy went behind a tree in the garden, looked up to heaven, and comforted Abraham by telling him that he had read on in the Bible story and knew that God would allow him to keep his son!

When Kold refused to hear the children reel off their lessons, or to teach them their catechism by heart, he was in trouble with the school authorities. He could not obtain any engagements as a teacher in a State school. He was considered a romanticist. Disappointed at the constant refusals, he decided to leave the country. He accompanied a clergyman who was going to the Middle East as a missionary. In Smyrna he earned his living first as a waiter, later as a book binder. After working there for five years, he succeeded in getting to Trieste with a skipper. Here he bought a two-wheeled handcart for his bookbinding tools, and trudged the 1,200 kilometres home on foot. As he still could not get a job as a teacher, he considered emigrating to America, for a time. But this came to nothing. With the new Constitution of 1849, the way seemed at last to lie open for freedom in school and church, and Kold saw his work as the realisation of Grundtvig's High School ideas.

Kold's High School

In 1851, Kold began – partly with his own hands – to build his little thatched high school on a small-holder's plot near Ryslinge on Funen, for money which he had saved in Smyrna, supplemented with a sum which Grundtvig and others had collected for him. The building still stands. This higher peasant school, like Uldum School, was an example where the initiative to its foundation came from the people themselves, and not from the State or from an academic elite. Not, however, that it was the local inhabitants who wanted the school, as had been the case at Uldum. Here it was a teacher, but a man of the people's roots, who was determined to have his own school, where the possibilities for this were present.

Kold visualized something in the nature of a continuation school for newly confirmed young people, because »18 year-olds belong to the rogue age, and are already less receptive to the impressions of poetry. It is the age when they are interested in buying watches and pipes. They are beginning to go courting, and a dull view of human life has already set in . . .« He disagreed with Grundtvig, who believed that 18 should be the minimum age for High School attendance. »No,« said Kold, »as I understand the matter, my opinion is the only correct one. I have always been convinced of my case, even when I was wrong.« And Kold was wrong. Later he was himself in favour of High School pupils being at least 18 years old.

According to his plan, the subjects taught at his High School were to be world history, scripture and Church history, Danish history, Nordic mythology and Danish poetry, as well as the ordinary subjects such as reading, writing and arithmetic.

In 1853 he moved his school to Dalby and the revivalists in the Kerteminde district. But their opponents regarded his activity with the greatest scepticism. They tried to persuade the peasants that it was practical knowledge and material development they needed, more than listening to Kold, for whom concrete skills took second place. They therefore sent petitions to the Government and the County Council, to refuse Kold any High School subsidy. In 1859 they got Lumby Farming School started near Odense. This was supposed to act as a counter-attraction to Kold's school. But in spite of abundant contributions from the State and the County, Lumby School did not last long.

From 1862 until his death in 1870, Kold was in Dalum near

Odense, where he had built a High School »like a castle« (Kold's own expression). Here he was the first of all the High School men to carry out his favourite idea for a High School for both men and women. In his last years he had 70 young men in the winter and 50 girls in the summer months.

Kold's High School was independent of the State. But he received a modest sum in State support right from the first year of the school, and sent in a report every year to the Ministry of Ecclesiastical Affairs and Public Instruction. From these reports and from the visits of the vicar of the parish, we know that lessons were also given in physics, chemistry and surveying, even though in Kold's opinion these were subjects of secondary importance. He left them to an assistant teacher. There were lessons from morning to night, only interrupted by meals. »The pupils are not mature enough for much independent work, particularly not on their arrival, and the exercises in mechanical skills are no more the object of the school than that of the pupils,« Kold wrote in his report to the Ministry.

When the spirit moved him, there was breathless silence among his listeners, but it was through conversation that Kold exercised the greatest influence on his pupils. In the evening he came into the commonroom to them, sat down on a bench and chatted with them. The answers he gave to the questions they put to him were usually accompanied by examples from his personal experiences. In this way he tried to rouse them to spiritual life and love for God and their neighbour.

In the 1860's, when he had built up a large school, there were always many visitors from outside. Amongst others, the pupils' parents. They came to sit in at his lectures. They had seen that their children had been completely changed by their stay at his High School. As they belonged to the religious revivalist circles, the fact that he had defied the State, and the local and school authorities, particularly appealed to them.

Grundtvig and Kold

After his death, Kold soon became a legendary figure. Few men in the history of Denmark stand out with such straightforward, concentrated strength. Whilst Grundtvig had great visions, Kold was the practical, working schoolmaster. Grundtvig understood that no one but Kold could talk so simply and directly to the young peasants. Here the living word could come into play. He regarded Kold as the best High School man in the country.

Kold's High School work was aimed at providing an impulse to his pupils. During a conversation with a man who asked him what he really wanted to do with the young people, he took out his watch, wound it up, and said that what he wanted was metaphorically to wind people up so that they never stopped again.

Kold often sought counsel and advice from Grundtvig. He was greatly inspired by Grundtvig's ideas. But he interpreted them in his own way and with great originality. They had different High School views on important points, partly because they had dissimilar backgrounds with regard to mentality, milieu, teaching and development. But the fact that they shared the same purpose – to get a Folk High School established – hid from them another fact, that they based their schools on different foundations.

Kold was not very well read. He had not even read Grundtvig's High School writings from the 1830's and 1840's. He was a man of the word, and had himself received the deepest impressions through the living word. There was a gulf between Grundtvig's blueprint for Sorø School, and Kold's High School on Ryslinge Field. This was in reality created without a model. He gave his pupils readings both of Grundtvig's World History and Nordic Mythology, and his assistant teacher Jens Lassen Knudsen (from Rødding High School) taught Danish history. But as the years passed, his High School changed. Perhaps he found it too difficult to interest the young peasants in world history.

In his last years at Dalum High School he had found his final form. Whilst in his report for 1858 to the Ministry he had called his subject World History, this was now designated »Spiritual Life Enlightenment«. Even Danish history was dropped, for he told Knudsen's successor that it did not matter what he told them, so long as he made sure that the pupils did not get up to mischief! He withdrew from Grundtvig's High School viewpoint. From being historical poetic, his message became, to a greater extent, an exhortation to follow Jesus' example in frugality and brotherly love. The ideals he held up for his pupils were thrift, self-sacrifice and hard work. All of it illuminated by edifying, everyday, moralizing examples from daily life. It was not a Grundtvigian interpretation of Christianity. The parental authority and parental love which Kold's school represented – the father, teaching his children, or the fatherly schoolmaster – would teach the young to forsake all wicked tendencies. Kold was the story-teller, and his idea was that by telling the stories so that the young people identified themselves with the drama in the stories, »the life urge« could be channeled into actions »with a good purpose«. Kold always acknowledged his inheritance from the religious revivalists, and must in fairness be judged on the background of the times in which he lived.

For Kold, Christianity was the only background for folk teaching. In 1856 he made a comparison between the three High Schools, Rødding, Hindholm and his own school. »Rødding«, he said, »must develop warriors in defence against Germanization. Hindholm must produce warriors for the fight for equality and freedom against the landed overlords. My school, on the other hand, must form warriors for the everlasting struggle between life and death.« The aim was to be ready for the heavenly Paradise, not to work to improve earthly life, as was the aim of Rødding and Hindholm. They had not understood the heart of the matter. They aimed too low, because they only had short-sighted human targets. The idea of Rødding High School – to form a shield against Germanization – was very near to Grundtvig's High School view, but was evidently inferior in Kold's. He himself wished to carry on the struggle between life and death in the Christian sense. Whilst Grundtvig went in for a secularized High School, although, indeed, it should repudiate a biological and materialistic view of mankind, Kold wished to form life according to a Christian ideal at his High School. And he therefore said: »My work is like John the Baptist's. He prepared the way of the Lord; and I must prepare the way of His Church.«

It was not, therefore, enlightenment for life in Grundtvig's sense that mattered, primarily, to Kold. According to the short-hand notes of the speech he held at the Grundtvig Friends' meeting in Copenhagen in 1866, he said that he had to do with pupils »who were unable to receive enlightenment until they had been 'animated'. It is animation they need.« In fact, Christian revivalism! And he continued:

»If I had met folk like the students in Copenhagen, folk who could let themselves be enlightened without first being animated, I might perhaps have started enlightening without first animating, for that is easiest, in a way, but face to face with the folk I actually met, I was, as I have said, obliged to use a different procedure. I think, also, that the more one gets to know the Danish folk, the more one will realise that, both in and out of Copenhagen, they cannot really be enlightened unless they are first animated, or at all events, that it must accompany it, that they are enlightened and animated at one and the same time.«

This statement confirms that for Kold, revivalism to Christian life was the primary task. Enlightenment on folk life must take second place. Through animation – as he says further on in the speech at the friends' meeting – one could give the children and the young people »such a delight, urge and strength, that one could make them believe in God's love and Denmark's happiness, and therefore work as well as one's modest abilities allowed . . .«

For Grundtvig, a living Danish patriotism and enlightenment on the life of man created by God, in the mother tongue, was a necessary condition for Christian life. It could not be a task for Christianity to call forth Danish patriotism. Kold's High School, therefore, was not a Folk High School in Grundtvig's meaning of the term, but more a Christian revivalist school. Grundtvig gave folk enlightenment. Kold gave folk upbringing. But he did not want to make his High School into a church. He preferred dialogue to sermons.

Kold dedicated his life, with a rare fervency, to the establishment of *free schools* for children. They were independent of the State. Parents associations chose and paid the teachers. The child's natural joy should not be killed by dull teaching by rote and examinations. The child should not be examined, but should grow in love for and dependence on the teacher who made the good stories from Danish history and from the Bible live through his telling. »The children«, said Kold, »do not belong to the State but to their parents. Therefore the parents must understand that they have the responsibility not only for the children's temporal good, but to just as great an extent for their spiritual upbringing.«

He stressed the homely and trustful, the close relations between teachers and pupils. The whole atmosphere was one of the greatest simplicity. Kold and his assistant teachers even shared the pupils' dormitories, as long as he had only small numbers at his High School. There they lay, and carried on long conversations with each other across the pupils' beds!

Kold became the model people looked to. University men came to Kold to learn good High School practice. But none of the next generation of High School men dared imitate him direct.

Since Kold did not regard his ideas and struggles in a social, human context, he did not concern himself with any form of political social information to his High School. But with his revivalist words, always concrete and realistic in relation to each pupil, he acquired great influence on the political development of the coming period. It should not be forgotten that the politician who led the movement to abolish the privileged right of election which was introduced with the Constitution of 1866, Klaus Berntsen, and the liberal left-wing peasants' leader of the same period, the editor Jørgen Pedersen, Fyns Tidende, had both been pupils of Kold.

Rødding, Uldum and Kold's High Schools became the ideals for High Schools thereafter. Many High Schools were started later, as Uldum was started, when the desire arose among a circle of farmers with fairly large properties. There are High Schools which have been run on the same educational lines as Rødding High School in Høgbro's time, and lastly there are High Schools which were to a great extent inspired by the lines laid down in Kold's High School. Many High Schools have tried to unite Uldum's practical agricultural instruction with

Kold's introspective self-development gospel and Rødding's more outgoing folk enlightenment.

At the outbreak of war in 1864, there were 15 peasant high schools in all. They were very different from each other, from the Bjørnbak type of school with examinations for solid secondary education, and political awakening to the Kold type of Christian-national revivalist school. There was not much co-operation between them. None of the first High School men so much as dreamed of realising Grundtvig's idea of a great State High School at Sorø, even though they were inspired by his ideas on enlightenment. The peasant high schools were started on local initiative, most often by shares being subscribed among local people. And so, also, were many of the High Schools which were established after 1864.

The High Schools and the State

Even the very first High Schools received State grants, and after the 1849 Constitution came into force, the »Peasants' Friends« who had seats in Parliament, tried to get the grants increased. But when the State demanded the introduction of examinations as a condition of support, both the High School men at Rødding and Christen Kold protested strongly. They declared that examinations were incompatible with the character of their schools. The High Schools did not aim at education for a particular trade, but gave enlightenment of universal human character. But this very viewpoint aroused protests from other quarters. Many thought that it was first of all necessary to give Danish peasant youth a solid technical agricultural education. During the passionate debate which followed, they demanded that all forms of State aid should be withdrawn from the High Schools, and that it should be given to the technical schools alone.

In this debate a voice of the greatest importance was raised. It was that of the estate-owner Edward Tesdorph, one of the foremost leaders of Danish agriculture. He had often had agricultural pupils and underbailiffs on his estate who had been at

Rødding High School. It had struck him that many of these former pupils from Rødding went to Scotland to study beet growing, which at that time was very little developed in Denmark. In answer to the sharp criticism of the High Schools he put forward a strongly worded recommendation of State aid to Rødding High School, in the annual report of 1858 of the Royal Agricultural Society. It concluded with the words:

>It would be difficult to do our country a greater service than to give its enlightened sons in the farming class such an opportunity for higher spiritual development, which will influence the whole population favourably and fruitfully. We are dealing here with an institution which has already stood the test successfully. Here there is no question of projects, for we know how we are using our money. We know that they will return to us with high interest. We know that in reality we do our country a great service by supporting Rødding High School.

>Let me add that so far as I can judge, the states which I have visited outside Denmark would eagerly seize such a good chance as is offered here to refine the core of our country, the peasant class.«

This far-sighted estate-owner Tesdorph's authoritative words in the actual conflict had decisive influence on the State policy of aid. The cultural and historical poetic line was preserved as the basis for the technical agricultural institution. It is also noteworthy that it was not the Government nor the academic Civil Servants, but the people's representatives, who took the initiative in High School aid. And the High School men's firm stand led to the State giving up the demand for examinations.

In spite of the State aid, the High Schools enjoyed extensive freedom. The authorities did not even demand inspection regarding educational methods as a condition. From 1876, under the anti-progressive land-owners, it was another matter.

IV.

THE BREAK-THROUGH IN THE YEARS
AFTER 1864

The War and its Effects

An Indian, on a study tour in Denmark, when he heard of the great High School period after 1864 exclaimed: »Yes, I understand that the High Schools are children of the Danish Army's defeat at Dybbøl in 1864.« This is perhaps an over-simplification, but it is a fact that the defeat by the German great power had decisive influence on High School history.

The Three Years War after the Slesvig-Holsteiners' rising in 1848 did not lead to any relaxation in Dano-German relations. For instance, Danish diplomats had tried in vain to get the British Government to understand Denmark's interest in separating Slesvig, the northern part of which had a large Danish majority, from the purely German Holstein. England, like Russia, was opposed to the naval port of Kiel in Holstein falling into the hands of Prussia. Denmark must not therefore state its frontier to be the Ejder. But under the pressure of the national feeling in 1863, the National Liberal Government carried a proposal for a joint constitution for Denmark and Slesvig to the Ejder. Thus Denmark broke the Agreement with the Great Powers after the Three Years War, not to attach Slesvig more closely to Denmark than Holstein. Bismark exploited this. When the Danish Government refused to withdraw the decision, the war with Prussia and Austria began.

On the night of 4 February 1864, the Danish Army had to retreat from the Dannevirke position. On 18 April, the Dybbøl redoubt was stormed. On 29 June, the Prussians captured Als. The war had ended, with Denmark's irreparable defeat. At the Peace of Vienna, Denmark had to give up two-fifths of the monarchy, with one-third of its population. Even though the large majority of the population of Slesvig and Holstein together were German, between 150,000 and 200,000 Danish North Slesvigians came under German domination.

Skåne had been lost in 1660, and Norway in 1814, and now came the loss of South Jutland. The time for national self-examination had come. One question arose, the whole gloomy perspective of which we can hardly imagine today. Could we carry on our political existence as an independent nation? As regards foreign policy, this must depend upon the fact that the one Great Power would not allow the other to seize the country. And in addition to the other resources which were lost during the revision of 1864, there was also the spiritual loss: the people's self-confidence.

The National Liberals' Ejder policy had suffered shipwreck. It had led to 1864. But they themselves explained the catastrophe by claiming that with the democratic Constitution of 1849, ordinary, uneducated men had risen too high. Denmark's salvation lay in her humbling herself and – as one of their leaders said – handing over the government to »the gifted, the educated, and the rich«. The National Liberals and some of the Peasants' Friends joined with the estate-owners in the party of the Right, and in 1866 they succeeded in carrying through a constitutional change, with privileged right of election, by which the estate-owners became the power in the *Landsting*. The right of election to the *Folketing* – the more democratic House of the two – remained unchanged, however. Here the Liberal Farmers' left wing won a solid majority, corresponding to its majority in the population. This formed an irreconcilable opposition against the estate-owners' government. A bitter constitutional struggle was beginning.

The Great High School Period

The war had not been an economic catastrophe. The destruction and the loss of human life had not been very great, and financially the country had been able to shoulder its effects. During the years following 1864, with good market conditions for agriculture, and the political trends in the farming classes which were strengthened by the constitutional struggle, one High School was established after another. In the years 1865–69, 85 new High Schools were started, and the number of pupils increased:

1865/66	729 pupils
1866/67	981 pupils
1867/68	1541 pupils
1868/69	2071 pupils

The numbers of pupils after 1870 is recorded for every fifth financial year.[1] »High School frequency« is also given, i.e. the numbers of pupils in percentages of the total numbers of unmarried 20-year-olds in the whole country:

	1870/71	1875/76	1880/81	1885/86	1890/91	1895/96
Number of High Schools	52		64		75	
Number of Pupils ...	2283	c.4000	3509	3750	3976	5163
H.Sch. Frequency ...	8%	11%	10%	11%	11%	13%

The increase in numbers of pupils in the years after the war up to 1876/77, where the climax was reached for the time being, was the most marked and most constant increase that the Danish Folk High Schools had for many years to come. These

1. In the numbers of pupils up to 1895/96, the Statistical Department has had to give approximate calculations, owing to lack of material. Roar Skovmand's statistics in *The Folk High School in Denmark 1841–1892* are more reliable, but do not include all the years. It is only where Skovmand's book does not include the information, that the Department's statistics are used.

years are therefore rightly called the great High School period. At the beginning of 1870, 52 High Schools received State aid. In the years 1880/81-1894/95, an average of 15% of one year's 20-year-olds in the country districts went to High School, and a High School term meant a considerable economic sacrifice, when the farm hands' and maids' wages are taken into consideration. In the survey below, the charges for teaching, board and lodging are compared with the average year's wages on the farms (excluding board and lodging). For the young men, a High School course of five winter months is calculated; for the girls, three summer months. This was the usual practice right up to 1950, when co-educational schools were started.

	1872	1888	1892
Farm workers, year's wages	kr. 126	158	199
School charges (5 months)	kr. 150	150	150
Proportion of wages	119%	95%	75%
Maids, year's wages	kr. 69	110	126
School charges (3 months)	kr. 90	90	90
Proportion of year's wages	132%	82%	71%

One can see that in 1872 a High School semester cost more than the average year's wages. It was particularly expensive for the girls, and after 1870 it was usual for the High Schools to hold summer courses for girls from 3 May to 31 July. From 1869, however, a minority of needy pupils received aid for a High School course, in accordance with a special provision in the Budget. After 1883/84, the grants were increased to 20 kr. a month, out of the pupils' expenses of 30 kr.; and following the provisions for aid in the High School Act of 1892, still more needy pupils received aid.

In 1894, on the background of the Grundtvig Voluntary Congregations, the High Schools had consolidated their position among the rural population. From 1866 they were no longer called Peasant High Schools, but Folk High Schools. This emphasized not only that their teaching and enlightenment activity, through »the living word« from the platform and in the interaction between teachers and pupils lay on a level which was comprehensible to the man in the street. The designation »Folk High School« also underlined that they should be schools to strengthen the whole folk community. But the number of pupils from the towns in these years did not exceed 5% of the total. Industrialization did not begin until the last decades of the last century, and the towns were still small. Even in 1870, three-quarters of the population lived in the country.

The High Schools became predominately farmers' schools. But gradually more of the sons and daughters of small-holders went to High School, partly because the amounts of the allowances were increased, and partly because the Co-operative Movement, which also spread in those particular years, had proved especially favourable to the small-holders.

»What was lost without –«

When »the great High School period« is under discussion, it is not only the outward numerical attendance that is referred to. There is also the inner character, as it was formed in those years, when the Folk High School became the Grundtvig movement's form of expression among the awakening farming classes connected with the Liberal Left. But first and foremost it refers to the zeal with which the High School pioneers took up their task after 1864. The fact that the Grundtvig High Schools have received their present form is not only thanks to the legacy of Grundtvig and Kold, but also to the character which it received from the pioneers after 1864: men for whom the desire to mobilise all available energies to counter the effects of the defeat was a constant inspiration for their work.

The decisive factor was what 1864 came to mean to academic youth, since it was they who took up the national questions on Denmark's future. Here the Copenhagen student club *Little Theologicum* was the focal point. It was from here that the most outstanding High School men came in the years that followed. They used to meet in the young divinity student Ernst Trier's room. In 1865 he started Vallekilde High School. Among other members we find Ludvig Schrøder the same year as Principal of Askov High School, and from 1866 Jens Nørregaard as Principal of Testrup High School.

What brought these gifted young theologians together was their membership of the Grundtvig movement. The course of the war and the peace had certainly brought great disappointments, but just as Grundtvig preserved his hopes for Denmark's future, so did his apprentices. 1864 must not be allowed to end in unavailing heroism. Like the soldiers who stood fast in Dybbøl's shattered redoubt in defiance of superior forces, they stood fast in the hope of Denmark's resurrection. Their hopes were fed by the belief that there were great unused treasures lying dormant in the peasants' low-ceilinged rooms – treasures which should be minted and lifted up into the light of day. This would more than compensate for the national values which 1864, with its harsh revision, had destroyed. They made the poet's words on the work of reconstruction after 1864, »what was lost without shall be won within«, the aim of their work.

The High Schools after 1864 became beacons on the peasants' way forward to equality with others. They gave them full compensation for the secondary schools in the towns. They met their need for enlightenment, which arose because of their growing political responsibility in the democracy which the Constitution had introduced, and they supported their efforts in the establishment of an independent rural culture. But even without the loss of South Jutland, the Folk High Schools would certainly have had wind in their sails during those years. The same occurred in Norway, Sweden and Finland.

The Critical Revision Men

In the period between the two Slesvig wars, most young university men had received their opinions in political and national questions from the National Liberal speakers at the university, in parliament and in the press. Amongst the few who remained critical towards everything the students sang and shouted »Hurra!« for, was Viggo Hørup, for whom 1864 was the natural consequence of the national student arrogance. He held the military type of higher university men and officers unmercifully to the hard fact: the defeat in 1864. He went in for a democratic, unromantic, anti-militaristic people's government, and his ideas received support not only in the academic world, but also in large sectors of the farming classes.

Within the student world there is good reason to mention the debating club, *The Band,* with the literary historian Georg Brandes. He was a National Liberal, it is true, but he had more critical sense than usual among the students of the time. On him, 1864 had the effect of tearing the bandage from his eyes. He was critical of the prevailing romanticism, and the National Liberal leaders' talk of Denmark's greatness. After his return from long travels abroad, he gave a number of lectures in 1871 at Copenhagen University. His purpose with these was to lead his countrymen to revise their self-satisfaction as a nation, and the way he took was to shed new light over the Danish folk by comparing them with the leading European nations. The conclusion which he reached was hardly flattering for us: whilst the great European cultural peoples had been busy advancing for a generation, we had stood still in naive self-satisfaction, educated by our poets to see ourselves in our Danish and Nordic forefathers' flattering reflection. Whilst Grundtvig High School folk after 1864 wished to confirm the young in this belief, *he* brought Christianity and the accepted moral norms up to debate.

At about this time, his friend, the poet J. P. Jacobsen, translated Darwin's *The Origin of the Species,* according to which men are descended from animals, and in the novel *Niels Lyhne* the poet described a man who slowly gained strength to live his life as a free-thinker. At the Grundtvig High Schools this book was for many years on the black list.

The Europeans, as the Hørup/Brandes school of thought was called, wished to lead the European cultural stream in over Denmark. They built on the ideas of the French Revolution, did homage to aesthetics and belles lettres, and with the daily paper *Politiken,* started by Hørup, they also made themselves felt in the press. They left their mark on a whole generation of university men: lawyers, doctors and teachers at the higher educational institutions. But there was something aesthetic and intellectually arrogant over these radicals' appearance, which was utterly alien to the peasants. In addition, their pessimistic view of the individual and the future of the motherland was the direct opposite of the Grundtvig High School folk's bluff faith in the future.

Ludvig Schrøder and Askov

What the students in *The Band* lacked, in deeper folk understanding and a positive attitude to national things, was supplied by the Folk High School men from the *Little Theologicum*. Among them, Ludvig Schrøder came to fill a central position. Under him, Askov High School, after an extremely modest beginning, became the Danish Folk High Schools' flag ship and model, which people in the other High Schools looked up to. Askov was carried forward by his desire to unite the two streams from Rødding and Christen Kold – unite enlightenment with the Christian animating and reviving word.

After the loss of South Jutland, Schrøder moved, with two assistant teachers, to Askov, three kilometres north of the 1864 frontier, to begin his High School career in a rented thatched one-storey house. They expected, however, that this would only be for a short time, and then they would move back to Rødding. After 1864 and up to 1870, there was considerable optimism as regards revenge on Germany with the help of France, but the war of 1870–71 wrecked these hopes.

The school opened on 3 November 1865 with 30 pupils, but later more joined them, so that in the first winter there were 42 pupils in all. For the first two winters, a number of the pupils had to live outside the school, because of the lack of space. But Schrøder was not idle. During the summer 1866, a house for 12–15 pupils was built. In 1868 the two buildings were bought, with the adjoining land; and in addition a low cheap building with a boarding roof was erected as dining room and dormitories, so that 40 pupils could live in the buildings with the two teachers. This meant a great deal for a life of comradeship.

The school work was carried on in cramped quarters. The first winter there was only one schoolroom, where all the lessons were held. There was more room for independent study, however, as they built on. 36 of the 54 weekly school hours were devoted to lectures. These all took place during the morning. In the afternoon there was writing, arithmetic, drawing, geometry, surveying etc.

But though the outer framework of the school could not be compared with conditions at Rødding, the number of pupils rose steadily from year to year. In 1869–70 the six-month winter course was already attended by 86 young men, and in the summer of 1870 there were 68 girls. Gradually more teachers were engaged, and the number of subjects increased: English, German, Norse, and mathematics – all voluntary subjects. The winter of 1876–77 brought 197 pupils. About half of them were former High School pupils, and of these 24 had been at Askov. The intake was so large that many applicants had to be refused, and while during the first five years the school had had a local character, from the middle of the 1870's pupils came from the whole country and from many different occupations. A growing number of them were over 25 years of age. There were always pupils from other Nordic countries, particularly from Norway.

Ernst Trier and Jens Nørregaard

Ernst Trier was the second of the influential Grundtvig High School men who had come from the *Little Theologicum*. He came from a Jewish home, the son of a rich timber merchant in Copenhagen, whose children had been baptized. At the university he studied divinity, and he attended Grundtvig's church at Vartov. With Grundtvig's encouragement he decided to take up High School work in Vallekilde in north-west Zealand. The circles which backed the foundation of this High School were in high degree politically aware. They maintained that it was important for the farmers to receive the enlightenment they needed, to be able to take part in the constitutional struggle. It was »not enlightenment which would make its bearer rise above ordinary folk and take up a hostile attitude to them, not enlightenment which would puff them up«.

Trier rented the main room in a farm as a schoolroom. 29 pupils arrived for the opening meeting on 1 November 1865. They had their meals at the farm, but were quartered here and there in the village. A year later, the school had already acquired its own building, an exact copy of Kold's High School in Dalum, with pupils' rooms, and the school building was enlarged as the number of pupils increased. In the winter 1872/73 the school had 110 pupils, and in the 1880's nearly 200. The summer school, at its height, had a similar number of girls. Vallekilde High School was thus the largest to date in the country.

A gymnasium was attached to the school, where physical training teachers were trained, and in Trier's last years, a department for artisans and one for sailors and fishermen was started.

Jens Nørregaard, like Schrøder, had originally intended to become a university lecturer. As there were folk in the Århus district who wanted a counter-weight to Lars Bjørnbak's secondary school type of examination school in Viby, he came to Testrup, near Århus, with a friend, Christoffer Baagø, who also belonged to the circle around the *Little Theologicum*. He himself said of this: »None of us expected material advantages from this work, but simply to be able to manage, living in very rough conditions. We both thought that after about ten years we would be able to leave this work and transfer to the priesthood.« It would turn out differently.

Nørregaard built Testrup High School at his own expense, and it opened on 1 November 1866 with 18 pupils. The school quickly grew, and reached about 100 pupils for each course. It was not until 1870 that he arranged to have the pupils living at the school. Later, he had to admit that this arrangement was greatly preferable:

»Daily life together, with its hundreds of points of contact and opportunities for influence, learning good manners, and supervision are of such value as a basis, that I can hardly imagine it stopped without having to halve the benefit of a school term for the pupils and satisfaction for myself.«

54

Ernst Trier understood that for a High School which gave its pupils preparation for life, lectures and other direct educational forms were not enough. He introduced gymnastics as a normal part of the time table.

The start of the gymnastics movement was in 1864. Its growth in the years after the defeat was conditioned by the work for reunion with the lost districts of Slesvig which were Danish-speaking. Gymnastics were introduced in the many rifle clubs which sprang up at that time. We could not believe that we could win North Slesvig back gratis. But gymnastics were only a side-line to rifle practice and other weapon exercises, and these were considered part of a national popular rising. Gymnastics gradually acquired a more important role in the rifle clubs, as it was realised that this too was valuable for the training of Danish youth in defence of the mother country. Training consisted mostly of drill, and most of the physical training instructors had an army training.

Up to 1880, the High Schools had not really followed this tendency, although at Vallekilde High School, for example, there were drill rifles and hookers hanging above the »long benches« on the wall of the »Viking hall«. But in 1884, Ernst Trier introduced Pehr Henrik Ling's Swedish gymnastics, and at the same time, the school gymnasium was opened. Trier thought the Ling gymnastics considerably more attractive than the military type of drill. He expressed himself in enthusiastic terms on the new gymnastics:

»The fact is that these Swedish physical exercises are not at all for training in some cause or other, such as warfare . . . The point is in reality that the use of physical exercises in general will penetrate our whole country and become a national cause.

In the event of war, it will then be proved that they have contributed to the development of courage, stamina and skill in the use of weapons. But in peace time it will lead to our youth gradually being guided to find the best form of recreation, by meeting together for what we have already begun here in Denmark, which could well be called 'free play', corresponding to the sports which the old Norsemen cultivated with so much pleasure . . .«

As one can see, Ernst Trier emphasized that the physical training should be Nordic, and he stressed the importance of the body. He was the first to understand that if gymnastics were to become a national cause, their development should not be undertaken from a military aspect.

At about this time, women's gymnastics were introduced at the High Schools in Vallekilde and Askov. A Swedish gymnastics teacher, Sally Högström was called in, and Swedish gymnastics went from strength to strength all over the country, adjusted to Danish conditions and the Danish character. Most of the High Schools started gymnastics departments on the Vallekilde model, and the many village halls which were built from the middle of the 1880's were equipped with ribs. They could thus be used both for gymnastics courses and for the cultural arrangements which the comradeship of these courses made possible. The Ling folk gymnastics became a necessary basis for the High Schools' existence. It was from the village halls' »gymnasia« that the High School pupils were recruited who would later become pioneers in the Co-operative Movement. And without this gymnastics work, the High Schools would hardly have obtained their great hinterland among the youth of the countryside.

School Life and Teaching

Life at all the High Schools was marked by the greatest simplicity. It was a tradition that most of the teachers ate with the pupils – sitting at the ends of the tables. Kold's High School was the example which was followed, particularly by Schrøder and Trier, in the insistence that the pupils should not be torn away from their everyday customs. The main meals were eaten in country fashion, with a common dish of stew, one dish for four persons, each helping himself from the dish, with wooden spoons.

Generally, there were 4–10 pupils to each dormitory. Each brought »half bed linen«, as each shared a bed with another. There was a small table and one or two stools to each room.

Apart from this, the beds could be used to sit on, if the pupils had work to do. There was neither quiet nor heating. Usually only one schoolroom was heated, by a stove, but this room was usually too small for all the pupils at once, and very few used it. At a number of the schools there was also another schoolroom, intended for reading the newspapers and chatting. These were filled to capacity. The few who wished to read in the evenings to supplement their knowledge on a question they had heard treated in a lecture, could borrow the principal's own books. But he had plenty of them.

In those days there were also variations in the time table from one school to another, but the differences were not so great as they are today. Many Grundtvig High Schools had time tables corresponding closely to the one given below, from Grundtvig's High School in 1881:

  8.00: morning hymns
8.15–9: lectures (on legends, myths, proverbs, biographies, scripture)
 9–10: poetry readings
10–11: free
11–12: lecture on Danish history
12–14: dinner
15–16: writing (composition)
16–17: free
17–18: geography or physics
18–19: arithmetic

All the lessons in the time table were obligatory for all the pupils. The wealth of variety in the voluntary subjects, studied in groups today, was unknown at that time. Since the teaching was based on »the living word«, books were only used to a very limited degree. In his report to the Ministry for the school year 1880/81, Nørregaard wrote: »Textbooks are only used when the pupils themselves ask for them.« Ernst Trier only used textbooks for arithmetic. At some schools the pupils themselves bought Flor's anthology of Danish literature. It was seldom that there was a reference library of any size. Askov was the exception to this.

As one can see, history lectures had a central position on the time table. These lectures were more than talks; they were spiced with anecdotes, and adjusted to the comprehension of the pupils, in words from everyday speech. But the first generation of High School folk were masters in the art of story-telling. With their teaching of history, the listeners heard associations from ancient half-forgotten experiences. They met the Grundtvig view of history: history should not be fragmentary data, but the living narrative, through which a connexion was created between what was recounted and the hearers' own lives. An inner dialogue should be set in motion which could contribute to moulding their thinking and their attitudes in the future. When, for example, Ernst Trier spoke on Jewish or Christian history, his pupils could see their own development reflected in the lives of these peoples.

Similarly, history formed the basis for the Christian view of life, although it could probably not have stood up to modern criticism of sources. The Grundtvig pioneers' aim – incidentally in contrast to Grundtvig's own view of history – was to show how God himself intervened in events. The Grundtvig High School, like Kold, regarded their work as a John the Baptist calling. The High School should be the way to the Church.

But it was not only history that was narrated. Through the historical poetic High School versions of Nordic myths and legends, the pupils were given teaching for life, and for the life of the soul, and this mobilised the pupils' understanding of human and folk life, with a longer perspective than simply solving the questions of the moment. In the struggle between the Nordic god Thor and the Midgard serpent, a metaphor for evil, and with Loke representing cold reasoning, the young people's eyes were opened to the constant warfare between good and evil, truth and falsehood. Clothed in the imagery of the myths, ethics were far from dull moralizing. They were the voices of »the Nordic tribes« speaking. This gave the lectures both authority and fervour. It was a prophetic High School, strong in purpose, and the best High School men were able to let situations speak for themselves, without the use of a pointer.

High School folk of later times have sometimes found it difficult to accept the historical poetic High School. In their view, it was not right to use myths and legends almost as gospel parables. But it was not unnatural a hundred years ago, in the national romantic epoch. In addition, the young men and women of the time were stay-at-homes. They had not heard or seen much, but they were used to listening to the peasants' unwritten literature, tales of ghosts and spirits, omens of death and fire, wicked overlords, strong peasants, etc. Their minds were open and receptive, and the many lectures did not tire them.

The lecture hours started, traditionally, with community singing. The songs used were not the drinking songs or love songs of the times, nor part songs chosen for the melodies, but songs inspired by old heroic Nordic legends or Bible history, or historical songs, most of them written by Grundtvig. They were connected quite naturally with the historical poetic lectures. In 1891, the newly formed Association of High Schools and Agricultural Schools published the *High School Song Book*. In later revised editions, many of the historical songs have given place to nature lyrics.

The Folk High School's Work and Aims

At the fourth Nordic Church congress in 1871, Ludvig Schrøder spoke on the Folk High School's work:

»When a flock of young people are brought together at a school which has no examinations as its final aim, the question arises not only as to what we, the teachers, have to say, but also what the young people will answer. There, where the teachers' abilities and the pupils' thirst meet, at any time, there is the school's work.

»Perhaps the time will never come, when we can say: 'Now we have a complete programme'. In the course of time the programme must change as the population develops. And I hope that the Folk High School will not become an institution in the sense that it stands finished and done with, but I hope that it will be borne onward by the independent personalities who devote themselves to its service. If they are not fit for it, the work of the school will stop on its own.«

By laying down, thus, that the Folk High School had to adapt itself to the needs of the pupils, or – as he later expressed it – where the needs of the *people* met the teachers' abilities, Schrøder had given valuable directives. The pupils who came to the High Schools were wanting elementary school teaching. In this connexion, Nørregaard laid particular weight on independent work. He differed from the imitators of Kold, who despised concrete knowledge. Pupils also received technical agricultural instruction, but first they must be »awakened«. An example of the way in which the problem was tackled at Askov, from the first public folk meeting in 1865, is where Schrøder's lecture treated the old Nordic myth, »Idun's Coming to Asgård«, whereas one of his assistant teachers spoke of spavin in horses – in other words, a purely utilitarian lecture for farmers.

Schrøder's decision on the work of the Folk High School is still valid. This applies to his realistic description of its social actuality, his emphasis on the absence of a programme, so that any High School ideology was precluded, and his reference to the meeting between teacher and pupil (people).

His thoughts on the Folk High School received their most concentrated expression in the university aula in Christiania (the present Oslo) in 1872, when he was speaker at the invitation of the Norwegian poet Bjørnstjerne Bjørnson and the Norwegian Students Association. On that occasion he said that it was a great advantage to the Folk High School, that it had to begin under low cottage ceilings, and that it had met peasant youth on a primitive level. This meant that the teachers had to adapt themselves to folk. He emphasized further that it was the aim of the Folk High School to give all the young people in the country the privileges which had been reserved for students hitherto – freedom to live their genuine youth, where young people could look around them and try to realise themselves. The school should help the young person to »get a wider view of human life, so that he did not feel himself shut in in his village, but discovered the great life of mankind in the whole of the North, yes, in the whole circle of the globe.«

The Extended Askov High School

In connexion with the discussion on the relations between the classical academic education and the folk Dano-Nordic education, a demand arose in Grundtvig circles for advanced education on the basis of the Folk High School. This was encouraged by the desire of many High School pupils to acquire more knowledge than could be had during one winter term at a High School.

It was in this context that Grundtvig's idea for a High School at Sorø reappeared. In 1878 it was put forward by Jens Nørregaard. The existing High Schools, in his opinion, could not both guard the legacy from Kold and meet the need for more enlightenment. Only if the flower of youth received a more concrete education than that which the ordinary Folk High Schools could give, would the gulf between the intellectual educated classes and the broad masses be filled. For that reason he advocated a State High School.

His arguments had a cool reception in the Grundtvig farming circles. For them, the State represented the Right Wing land-owners, the great dragon, and a threat to freedom. They preferred an extended High School, founded with private contributions. The task must therefore be to expand Askov, which approached the Sorø ideal more closely than did any of the other existing High Schools.

And this was done. With enthusiastic support from many quarters, Schrøder decided from the winter 1878 to introduce advanced education at Askov. A certificate of general education was required for entrance to the extended High School, either in a report from an earlier stay at a High School or in some other way. The most important subjects were Nordic and world history (including political history, Church history, the history of literature, cultural history and the history of art), Danish, geography, mathematics, natural sciences and some knowledge of law. A new subject – conversation – was introduced, and special weight was laid on homework, with short essays.

During the winter there were already 60 pupils at the extended High School. Out of the pupils from the first six terms, about half came again the second year, and a number continued for a third winter, some of these to be trained as priests without a divinity degree for the emigrant Danish congregations in the U.S.A., or for the Danish congregations in the ceded South Jutland. But the hope that Askov could make an important contribution to the establishment of education on the academic level was dashed. There was not sufficient interest.

From the year 1879/80 the extended High School received a sum on the Budget each year, over and above the ordinary High School grants. They were able to fit up pupils' rooms to house 2–3 pupils, intended for those who wanted peace and quiet in which to do their homework. Classrooms were furnished for the new teaching staff.

One of these was the physicist Poul la Cour. He was appointed in 1878, to teach mathematics and physics. To have a natural scientist on the staff was a landmark in the history of the school. La Cour broke new ground. He treated his subjects from the historical point of view, building chronologically on the constantly increasing discoveries from the mathematicians and scientists of antiquity to our day. The teaching of the natural sciences became a link in cultural and spiritual history. In 1881 he prepared *Historical Mathematics*. Later *Historical Physics* was published, with the Askov teacher Jacob Appel as joint author.

Poul la Cour was a teacher of genius. He could make the most difficult subjects comprehensible to ordinary High School pupils with no particular preparatory knowledge, and both the historical mathematics and the historical physics gave them an excellent foundation for the understanding of ordinary mathematics and physics. At this point, when the »Europeans« and the Danish natural scientists attacked the High School folk, the young people were meeting a natural scientist who stood firmly on the old Christian foundation, even if his authority did not go unchallenged.

In 1882, Ludvig Schrøder engaged the poet Jakob Knudsen and the later so well-known principal of Frederiksborg High School, Holger Begtrup, to teach modern literature. But like the great majority of the High School folk of those times, these young theologians also believed that the naturalistic literary view of man, as determined by the absolute power of natural law, contained a danger which they must fight.

By the middle of the 1880's, interest in the Nordic myths weakened after philologists at Copenhagen University had cast doubt on the Nordic origins of the Eddas.

Years of Political Struggle

The High Schools had another side, opening on political life. They were all more or less actively engaged in the struggle for freedom and right, which was the Grundtvigian Leftist politicians' particular cause. However, they did not try to influence the pupils politically, direct, in their teaching, and they often disagreed on procedure and tactics, in the struggle of these years against the Right Wing's unparliamentary methods.

From the election in 1872 the Left Wing had a clear majority in the *Folketing* to which there was, after all, universal and equal suffrage, and the Left demanded that the King should choose his Ministers in accordance with the principles of parliamentarism for the *Folketing*. But the Right insisted obstinately that the provision in the Constitution that »the King is free to choose his ministers« meant the constitutional equal right of the *Landsting*. The *Folketing* could not have any prior right over the *Landsting*. The leader of the Right, the land-owner J. B. S. Estrup, who became Prime Minister in 1875, refused therefore to resign. The Grundtvigian Leftist politician, the former principal of Rødding High School, Sofus Høgsbro, described Estrup's government as »an open challenge and declaration of war against the *Folketing*«. In 1877 the struggle became more acute, when a conflict with the Left on grants to the Army made Estrup meet these expenses with a Provisional Finance Law.[1] This was stamped by the Left as a clear infringement of the Constitution, since the payment of these expenses had not been passed in constitutional form. A great many High School principals, with Schrøder and Nørregaard at their head, demonstrated by refusing to apply for State aid for their High Schools. The conflict

---

1. A provisional law is a temporary law issued by the Government alone. Section 25 of the Basic Law said: »In very special cases, the King, when Parliament has been dissolved, can issue provisional laws, which must not contravene the Basic Law of the Constitution, and should always be put before the next Parliament«. Such an emergency provision is to be found in most Constitutions – a crisis may arise when a responsible Government should act resolutely, without waiting for Parliament to meet. Estrup made use of it to dissolve Parliament, so as to issue a Provisional Finance Law.

blew over, however, when Parliament met again and a majority of the Left agreed to a compromise on the Finance Law.

In the years that followed, however, the Right had to submit to the Left cutting the Budget appropriations for military purposes, and in 1884 the Left won its greatest election victory to date. Opposition did not make Estrup any more amenable. He refused to submit to the military appropriations being cut down every year, and the Government therefore decided to take the money and the appropriations it wanted, by making a new Provisional Finance Law. Most of the High School principals resumed their protest against this unconstitutional procedure, but the Government replied by cutting out eight schools, including Askov, from the list of schools which could receive State aid. Nor could the pupils receive stipendia, if their principals took part in the rebellious Rifle Clubs directed against Estrup. Two of the principals were put in prison, and a »muzzle circular« forbade High School teachers from taking part in political agitation. But the former pupils from the High Schools and their friends formed supporting clubs. The High Schools received their State aid again, when the Right wing politician Mathias Steenstrup, who had been State Inspector of the High Schools from 1876, declared that the charges against the High Schools of political activity had no foundation in fact.

Eventually the conflicting parties became more conciliatory. In 1892 came the law on State aid to the High Schools and the Agricultural Schools. They had previously received subsidies on the annual Budget, but thereafter ministerial discrimination was made impossible. In 1894, political conciliation was achieved. Estrup stopped governing via provisional budgets, and in 1896 he resigned altogether from political life.

The Folk High School and the Towns

The workers in the towns generally felt unfamiliar with the refined village culture which was the work of the High Schools, but gradually they realised what these schools had meant for the social upsurge of the peasant classes. Some of those who later held leading positions in the Social Democratic labour move-

Rødding High School. The building on the left was the first High School in Denmark, from 1844. The building in the centre, of which only the gable is visible, was built by Ludvig Schrøder in 1863.

Odder High School.

Engelsholm High School. Formerly Engelsholm Castle, the manor house of the Engelsholm estate, near Vejle, built in 1593, with two storeys and four massive corner towers.

Krabbesholm High School. Formerly Krabbesholm Manor, near Skive. Two-storey building with 16th century tower. The wings are from a later date.

Esbjerg High School, grouped with individual houses.

Herning High School. The students are housed in the fifteen-storey sky-scraper; school activities are carried on in long one-storey buildings. At the top of the sky-scraper there is one flat for an artist and another for an author.

The Sønderborg Physical Training High School.

Brandbjerg High School near Vejle.

ment's information work had been at High School, before the turn of the century. They felt attracted in many ways by the High School form: the plain friendly tone, the comradeship and community singing. But they were and remained peasant High Schools in their eyes. They were Christian-national, whereas the Social Democratic labour movement was socially and internationally oriented.

In the last decades of the nineteenth century the critical scientific attitude to life won support among the workers. They were influenced by Georg Brandes, who had opened the windows for the radical cultural streams from abroad. In 1882, the *Student Association* was formed.

This became a meeting place for Brandesian university men. The same year the *Student Association's Evening Classes for Workers* was started. Teaching was given here both in practical subjects and in general educational subjects, and over 100 teachers gave their services gratis in their free time. The rush of applicants was far beyond their expectations. But of course this was not an actual High School. The boarding school form was lacking.

In 1891, the High School man Morten Pontoppidan started a High School in Copenhagen. Before it opened he emphasized that the school was not to be based upon any particular view of life: »Everything that smacks of sectarianism is incompatible with the High Schools' original idea.« He expected to have pupils both from the country and from Copenhagen. He chose both Grundtvig High School folk and men from the Student Association for his staff. But he too lacked pupils. After two years he had to give up.

Things went better for his good friend Johan Borup, who started his High School activities in Copenhagen at about the same time. He did not announce it as a »High School« – the name was compromised for Copenhageners – but as »advanced education for non-university ladies and gentlemen«, in general subjects. There was a good intake at Borup's day High School. Later it received the name *Borup's High School.* In 1891–92 the school was attended by 138 pupils, the year after, by 218, and after the turn of the century, over 400. From 1894 the school was already receiving a special subsidy on the Budget.

When in 1865 Ernst Trier started Vallekilde High School, he received support from the clergyman Vilhelm Beck, later the leader of the Home Mission. Trier was afraid, however, that this might be based on false premises, and it would later prove that his misgivings had some foundation in fact.

The Home Mission became the most widespread religious movement in Denmark apart from Grundtvigianism. Its aim was evangelical revival. At first the Mission folk and the Grundtvigians stood shoulder to shoulder to resist the sects, particularly the Baptists and Mormons. But gradually the differences between the Home Mission and Grundtvigianism became glaring.

In Home Mission circles, doubts arose on sending their young people to Grundtvigian High Schools. The Mission folk were very much opposed to the mentality and the form of comradeship at these schools. They demanded an austere, ascetic attitude to life, with no dancing, card playing or use of alcohol, and they differentiated sharply between »God's children« and the »world's children«. The Home Mission therefore decided to start their own High Schools. At the turn of the century there were 5 Home Mission High Schools: Nørre Nissum High School (1887), Børkop High School (1889), Horne High School (1891), Haslev High School (1891) and Rønde High School (1897). More were added later.

When the Home Mission High Schools were established, it was laid down that their aim was »to revive and nourish serious Christian life, and communicate useful knowledge«. The most important subject on the time table was not history, but Bible knowledge. The Bible was an important link in the school's daily work. Christian ethics and Mission lectures took a central place. In addition the pupils themselves held Bible readings in small groups, apart from the actual teaching. But in accordance with their aims, these schools were also strongly technical in character; they did not shrink from assigning and hearing homework, and lectures did not have such a dominant place on the time table as they did at the Grundtvig High Schools.

One Home Mission High School man defined the difference between the Grundtvigian and Home Mission High Schools as follows: »At the Grundtvigian High Schools one says: 'First the man, then the Christian.' We say: 'First the Christian, then one becomes a man.'« The Home Mission High School folk repudiated any sharp division between school and church, and declared that they recognized Kold's legacy more than did the Grundtvigians. Kold had regarded Christian revival as the most important aim of his school. But that was the only likeness there was, for Kold rejected the use of textbooks, and was uninterested in utilitarian informative education.

Like the first Grundtvig High School pupils, the pupils at the Home Mission High Schools varied considerably in age. About one-third were 18, and just as many were over 30.

There was no actual co-operation in the folk work in the country in general between the two movements. Whereas the village halls were the work of the Grundtvig High School movement, the Home Mission folk built mission houses, and turned their backs on the cultural work. During the struggle against the provisional laws, the Home Mission folk took up a passive attitude, as they also did in the intellectual struggle for Southern Jutland's return to Denmark.

The Effects of the High Schools

In judging the effects of the High Schools on the peasant classes in the first decades after 1864, the folklore expert, H. F. Feilberg concludes:

»In general, if I am to point to the mark of the High School work on the people . . . I should say that it has left traces in the education of the people, and that it has had an educative and civilizing influence. The peasants' previous desire to read has increased, countless much used libraries have been established, lecture clubs started, village halls built; I would add that the rifle clubs run exactly parallel with the High School movement; all in all, the average of intelligence among the people has been raised«.

Feilberg also points out that conversation between people in rural society had been raised to a higher level. Where, before, it had been about buying and selling, and superstitions, now one discussed topical questions. The tone had improved, homes had become prettier, working life and marriage had been refined.

As far as the purely practical effects on the rise of the peasant classes were concerned, it certainly meant something that most of the High Schools gave technical agricultural instruction. A course at both a High School and an Agricultural School was not usual, few farmers' sons took their matriculation examination, and if they did, they did not return to farming, and there were hardly any secondary schools. The High School pupils' educational background was only elementary schooling. But the High Schools had a large reserve of intelligence in their band of pupils.

However, it was a tradition-bound peasantry that sat and listened on the hard benches in the lecture rooms. It is well known that all over the world, the farming classes belong to society's conservative sector, as far as their attitude to what is modern and topical in society is concerned. Where the urban dweller is formless and untraditional, the peasant is guided by conventional thinking.

And yet the Danish peasants were certainly not as rigid as many other peasants in the nineteenth century. They showed themselves to be accessible to new ideas. Apart from the agrarian reforms in 1788, Grundtvig's ideas for the Folk High Schools contributed to this in high degree, for the High School men understood that the peasant did not in reality lack creative imagination, when he was faced with new and unusual problems. There were great latent possibilities, but first, a human awakening was necessary to shake the traditional beliefs. The fervent words, in historical poetic form, which rang from the High School rostra, met receptive minds. »The wisdom in the Nordic myths, as I heard them told at Askov in my young days, encouraged youth to action,« wrote one of Ludvig Schrøder's former pupils. That was the essence of his High School term in 1874/75. He transformed a neglected farm into a model one. Like so many others, he believed that the spiritual awakening received at the High School is converted into practical energy.

The Co-operative Movement

From 1880 onwards, Danish agriculture met serious competition from cheap corn imports from overseas and from eastern Europe. The fall in prices made many farms unprofitable, and production had to be converted to the export of animal products to the industrial countries, first of all Great Britain. The cost of this had to be met by the farmers themselves. But this conversion was made possible by co-operation in producer unions.

A start was made in Hjedding in West Jutland in 1882, when a group of farmers started the first co-operative dairy. This was the first step towards a co-operative dairy industry, with wide ramifications throughout the country. By 1890 there were already 679 co-operative dairies in Denmark. They were often started in districts where folk activity had paved the way. In 1887 the first co-operative bacon factory was started in Horsens by the High School man Peter Bojsen, and before 1890, co-operative bacon factories had been started in Kolding, Esbjerg and six other towns in Jutland and on the islands.

In these co-operative dairies and bacon factories, every member received a share of the profits in proportion to the size of his deliveries, but prices and methods of treatment were the same. All had equal rights. At the General Meetings, the small-holders and the land-owners sat on the same bench, and their voices had absolutely equal authority and force. Votes were taken per head – not per head of cattle. The members shared joint ownership of the production plants, and the capital was raised by loans against security in their joint liability, as was the case in the co-operative stores with the purchase of fertilizers, feeding stuffs and seed.

The democratic principle of equality did not mean, however, that competition was eliminated. Those who delivered the best milk to the dairy, and those who delivered the best pigs to the bacon factories received the best prices per kilogramme. And it was always a matter of pride to be in the first category, when quality was judged.

The importance of comradeship and healthy competition was in the old co-operative farmers' blood, from the gymnastics in the village hall, where the young farmers and farm hands used to train without differences of status. And above the desks at home in the living room hung the group photograph of the pupils at the High School, and urged responsibility for the whole. The High Schools' influence was of an indirect kind, however. No instruction was given on the Co-operative Movement. This subject was not to be found on the time table. But through his narratives from the nation's history the High School man sought to awaken each pupil to the understanding that he was not simply an individual, but a living part of the whole. Thus he was called to action and co-operation, and the cultivated democracy in the farmers' co-operative unions became a natural sphere of action.

Most of the pioneers in the Co-operative Movement were influenced by the High School. During the debate on the Budget for 1888/89, Ludvig Schrøder, who was then a member of the *Landsting*, declared: »In those districts where the dairies are going well, one will find former High School pupils, who have put the co-operative dairies on their feet, and one will also find old High School pupils who serve as dairymen . . .« In 1897, 47% of the chairmen of the dairies had been at a High School.

The Years of Break-through at an End

In the years between 1890 and the turn of the century, several of our large High Schools (such as Askov, Vallekilde and Testrup) celebrated their 25 years jubilees. These ended with, and so to speak came together in, the 50 years jubilee in 1894 of the first Folk High School in Rødding. In connexion with the High School jubilees, it was obvious to dwell on the national struggle in South Jutland. The 30 years remembrance of 1864 almost coincided with the 25 years anniversary of the foundation of great national enterprises such as the Heath Company (1866) which reclaimed and transformed heathland into new arable land, the United Steamship Company (1866) and the Great Nordic Telegraph Company (1869). All signs of a nation full of vitality. This nearly eclipsed the losses of 1864.

Then, through all the cheerful festive tones, sounded a penetrating, grating voice. It was Georg Brandes'. In 1894 he gave a lecture in the Student Association »On National Feeling«. Here he expressed himself anything but appreciatively on developments in Denmark since 1864, and drew a gloomy picture of the future, presumably as an antidote to the bright pictures of those years. There was considerable protest, and Brandes met several of the Grundtvigian leaders, such as Nørregaard, for a hot debate at the Student Union. The meeting calls to mind the famous scene from the Edda poem on Ægir's feast, where Loke enters into an acrimonious duel of words with the gods who are in festive mood, and where Thor comes to shut the mocker's mouth, and attacks him with his hammer. Loke continues to remind the gods, particularly Thor, of unfortunate experiences, which give rise to forebodings for the future: Ragnarok, which he continues to prophesy for them. Thor finally gets him driven out with his lifted hammer, and Loke flees, but the festive mood is spoiled. Not the will to fight and to work, however.

But in spite of such unpleasant attacks from without, the national romantic home front held unbroken within the High School movement. Apart from this, no direct collisions took place between these two partly opposed movements. The critical »revision men« and the affirming believers divided the country between them.

As a new development, the *Association of High Schools and Agricultural Schools* started its first university course in 1894. Respected representatives of a number of sciences gave lectures for older and younger High School folk. These courses were held for one or two weeks every autumn in Copenhagen. Later the courses were held every other year, and transferred to one of the larger High Schools or Agricultural Schools.

As already pointed out, the Folk High Schools that had gradually come into being did not altogether correspond with Grundtvig's original plan. He had not anticipated the establishment of many small schools, started on private initiative. He could hardly have foreseen the very time-consuming work with the elementary subjects, written Danish and arithmetic, or that a term at a High School would only last 3–5 months.

71

V.

1900–1920

In Smooth Waters

The High School concept had won through. And the words
»High School« stood for the idea of a Grundtvig High School. It
was for the next generation to harvest the fruits of the pioneers'
work.

The High Schools were no longer at the front, without cover.
The law of 1892 on State aid, and a compact Liberal majority in
Parliament stood guard over their liberty. The Right, which had
tried to control their freedom, suffered its greatest electoral defeat in 1901. The King finally yielded to the parliamentary
majority, and appointed a Liberal government. Parliamentarism became the constitutional practice.

With this change of political system, farmers became Members of the King's Council. The aim of Grundtvig's great High
School idea had been fulfilled, and from 1901 High School folk
or former High School pupils have sat in nearly all Danish
governments.

During the years of break-through there had been a great deal
of resistance to overcome, before young people could attend
High School. Their friends made fun of them. Their parents
opposed them. It was not unusual for an old farmer to grumble
at how demoralizing the schools were: the young people simply
lazed there, and then when they came home, they subscribed to
the *High School Paper* [1] and wanted to express opinions! But they

---

1. The High School Paper (*Højskolebladet*), the journal for Danish folk enlightenment, and particularly widely read i Grundtvigian High School circles, was founded in 1876.

came to the High School determined to get something great, yes, the greatest possible value from their course, even though it gave no examination certificates, and even though they had to make great economic sacrifices for it.

Now it was different. Young people were often strongly encouraged by their parents, or they went to High School because it was the done thing among their comrades in the local gymnastics club.

In the first years after 1864, the High School pupils had heard or read little or nothing about what was going on outside their own narrow circles. Their need and urge towards light and emancipation was met by the corresponding urge of a teacher to bring them the light and emancipation which had once been his own great experience. For it required a strong motive force to bring gifted young university men, for whom access to government positions stood open, to take up the uncertain High School work. They too could be laughed at by their comrades. A strong will was needed, if all this was to be overcome. But when − scorning a secure future − they stood face to face with the young people, they burned with fervour and self-sacrifice. And the words of enthusiasm that rang from the rostra roused the young people to follow the ideas which they saw that the speakers had staked their lives to realise.

After the years of break-through, the life and folk enlightenment which the Folk High School had to offer was not so completely new as it had been in the past. From their homes and schools, from newspapers and lectures, many were familiar with them already. The influence of the High Schools could hardly continue to be such an overwhelming experience: the leap from darkness and constraint into light and freedom. The High School term was no longer comparable to an awakening, joyful morning hymn which was the start of a new people's day. This new day was already somewhat advanced.

The awakening that may have taken place did not occur in connexion with Grundtvig's humanity and Christianity, but rather with the religious pietistic Home Mission schools, and socially within the politically-minded circles in the form of Socialism and Henry George's Single Tax Movement. This did not mean that the period after the turn of the century was inferior for the Folk High Schools. But it was different. And the young people became more emancipated through their stay at the High School. Now they could also talk of other things than harvest prospects and potato lifting.

The High Schools and the Intake of Pupils

The number of High Schools and the intake of pupils in the years 1900–1920 can be seen from the following table, which, except for the year 1919/20, only gives the figures for every fifth financial year, like the survey on p. 47:[1]

	1900/01	1905/06	1910/11	1915/16	1919/20
Number of High Schools	74	71	79	70	57
Number of pupils	5362	6689	6707	5623	8097
High School frequency[2]	13%	15%	14%	11%	14%

The growth of the High Schools culminated in 1911. In the years 1911–19 only one High School was started, while in the same period 23 were closed. It was particularly the small schools for individual districts which had difficulties, owing to the War and the high cost of living. In that period about two-thirds of the schools were owned by the principals, who ran them at their own account and risk, in accordance with the liberal views of the day. The same was the case if the principals had rented the schools from private companies in which High School supporters from the area had subscribed shares.

1. The Statistical Department's statement on the numbers of pupils for the years 1905/06–1935/36 contains a fault in calculation, as pupils are also included who continued their courses after the end of the financial year on 31 March and for a month into the following financial year. Since some High Schools, such as Askov High School, had six-months winter semesters to 1 May, this double count gives a total of pupils which is a little too high for the years in question.
2. For »High School frequency« cf. p. 47.

The numbers of pupils reached their height in 1919/20, at the same time as the number of High Schools reached their lowest number to date. The reason was partly that many had postponed attendance at a High School until after the War, and partly because North Slesvig's population was included in the census. Pupils from farms constituted 70–75%; pupils from working class homes in town only 3%. Except for Askov and Vestbirk High School, the large High Schools, covering the whole country, which had more than 250 pupils at the summer and winter courses together, all lay on the islands. Among them were Frederiksborg High School, Vallekilde High School, Ollerup High School and Ryslinge High School. The eight largest High Schools together had 40% of all High School pupils. The other High Schools were therefore small. Competition led to the young people going to the High Schools which were already large, and had many former pupils to speak for them. Their principals were well known as lecturers and readers throughout the country. The small High Schools on the other hand worked in depth, with their homely atmosphere.

Teaching Staffs

The High Schools, then as now, had both permanent staff who lived at the school, and temporary staff. As no particular examination certificates were demanded of High School teachers, they were a motley crowd. But that was the special charm of the teaching staffs. Besides the university men and those who had graduated from teachers' colleges, there were both men from agricultural schools and a number who had had one or two semesters at Askov, or a gymnastics training, as their background. After the turn of the century, the number of teachers with divinity degrees decreased somewhat, although there were still many for whom High School teaching was a stage on the way to a parson's incumbency. But at the same time, the number with academic degrees from other faculties increased. The greatest increase, however, was that of staff with teachers' college diplomas.

The Swiss High School man, Fritz Wartenweiler, who taught for a time at Ryslinge High School, and who was one of the foreigners who knew the Danish High Schools best, summarized his impressions of that generation's High School men as follows:

»I came to know many different types of High School and also came into contact with principals and teachers of the most dissimilar character: highly educated theologians and natural scientists, plain men and women, enthusiastic, energetic politicians and leaders in the agricultural field, orthodox Grundtvigians and free thinkers – and in spite of all the differences I noticed a unity which could only be the result of a deep stir. I saw with astonishment that some of the best men in the country had engaged themselves in the service of this cause. Here was one who had given up a brilliant university career in order to serve the people direct. There was another who had worked his way up from beneath, through all the farm worker's difficulties, and had overcome the irregular form of his development in order to be able to help folk of his own category better. There was nowhere any strict organisation, nowhere a decided leader, but on the contrary, a great number of independent units, intimately connected into a harmonious whole.«

This description of the High School teachers' heterogeneous flock is still valid today.

But the Folk High School was also exposed to criticism. There were those who thought that its aim was too introspective, that it was mostly a matter of enlightenment for life in home circles and in the individual soul – a Christian moralizing enlightenment for daily life.

Among the critics were, for example, Henrik Pontoppidan and Jakob Knudsen, who both knew the High School from the inside.

Pontoppidan, who had been a teacher of natural history at his brother Morten Pontoppidan's High School in 1878–81, accused the Grundtvigian High School folk of lack of solidarity with ordinary people. He found that »High School life, with its constant Sunday atmosphere and everlasting songs of praise« did not harmonise well with the reality outside the High School's narrow world.

Jakob Knudsen criticised the High School from quite a different viewpoint. In a lecture in 1904 he said that far too many High School men »took the wrong path in imparting knowledge«. This might pass. But it was worse that still more »plodded along the broad highway of moralizing and preaching«. On the other hand, in his opinion, the High School teaching was good when it made the great figures of history live, and that in itself would have a moral educative influence on the pupils.

The Pioneers

After the change in the political system in 1901, political interest flagged somewhat. Fewer High School men went over to political activity. They turned their gaze inwards, to the work in their own schools and the work of enlightenment generally. Several of the High Schools changed their principals. Like Trier, Nørregaard and Schrøder were replaced now by men who had themselves been at a High School and could carry on its traditions. Besides Holger Begtrup at Frederiksborg High School, it was men like Jacob Appel at Askov High School, Thomas Bredsdorff, who founded Roskilde High School in 1907, and Alfred Povlsen, Ryslinge High School, who represented the High Schools in those years.

Jacob Appel was born at Rødding, where in proper Grundtvig spirit he was taught at home by his father, a parson. At the age of 16 he went to Askov, where he remained for three years, making it his second home. After this he educated himself in free studies in mathematics and physics at Copenhagen University and the Polytechnic Institute, but without taking an examination. One was against examinations in the Grundtvig school circles Appel came from! In 1890 be became a teacher at Askov High School, where every summer he led a three-months summer school for High School teachers, and in 1906 he became Schrøder's successor. Appel's subjects were the natural sciences. He was an excellent pedagogue, and he could deal with the world outside with the authority accruing from his position as principal of Askov High School. In the years 1910–13 he was Minister of Ecclesiastical Affairs and Public Instruction, and 1920–24 Minister of Education, from 1922 also Minister of Ecclesiastical Affairs in the Liberal government of the day.

Alfred Povlsen had been a pupil under Nørregaard at Testrup

High School, and had then trained at a teachers college. In the years 1884–1929 he was principal of Ryslinge High School. In the years of the provisional laws he was one of the leaders among the High School folk who demonstrated against the unconstitutional policy of the Right, and this resulted in his losing his State subsidy. Ryslinge High School thrived, however, and from 1910–1920 had about 400 pupils every year. For a number of years Povlsen held the position of chairman of the Association of High Schools and Agricultural Schools, at the head of the many who declared that it was only in the lectures that one found the »soul of the school«.

Thomas Bredsdorff, as a vicar's son, was deeply rooted in the Grundtvig way of thinking, and like Appel he had been a pupil at Askov High School. As a divinity student in Copenhagen he was influenced by the Brandes outlook, although he never adopted it. In 1907–1922 he was principal of Roskilde High School, which became one of the largest High Schools in the country. One of the guiding principles in his teaching was that the Folk High School should not influence its pupils so that they echoed their teachers. To develop their independence he introduced hours for conversation in the High School time table. He hoped to get into conversation with the urban workers, but he never really succeeded in this.

School Work

To give an impression of the teaching at the High Schools after the turn of the century, a typical time table, for the winter 1901/02 is given below:

	Monday	Tuesday	Wednesday
8–9	Geography	Geography	Danish history
9–10	Danish	Danish	Danish
10–11	Gymnastics	Gymnastics	Gymnastics
11–12	World history	World history	World history
14–15	Danish history	Danish history	⎰ Drawing and
15–16	Writing	Natural history	⎱ surveying
16–17	Arithmetic	Arithmetic	Arithmetic
17–18		Readings of early and modern literature	

	Thursday	Friday	Saturday
8–9	Geography	Danish history	Geography
9–10	Danish	Danish	Danish
10–11	Gymnastics	Gymnastics	Gymnastics
11–12	World history	Church history	Church history
14–15	History of literature	⌠Drawing and	Danish history
15–16	Natural history	⌡surveying	Hygiene
16–17	Arithmetic	Arithmetic	Arithmetic
17–18	Readings of early and modern literature		

The main emphasis was still laid upon the lecture form. At most of the High Schools almost half the weekly 48 hours of teaching were reserved for history, Danish and literature.

The increasing importance of gymnastics was also noticeable in the teaching plan. Practically all the pupils took part in gymnastics lessons. It was insisted that rational physical exercises did not only develop the pupils physically, it also increased their mental capacity.

At Askov High School more stress was laid on mathematics and the natural sciences than at other High Schools, and here lessons were also given in German and English. On the whole, the High Schools were changing over to more modern working methods of teaching. Appel and Bredsdorff also wished the pupils to be familiar with the use of books, and many High Schools acquired reference libraries. But the living word was still common to them all, as well as singing, comradeship between the teachers and pupils, and the homely atmosphere.

Agricultural departments were often introduced at the High Schools. This technical instruction was at the cost of the cultural subjects, but could be a vital necessity for the High Schools, because of competition with the technical colleges. Only a minority among the young men could afford to go to both High School and agricultural college, and the agricultural college students increased from year to year. The competition between the High Schools themselves was just as keen. It was a great temptation in advertisements to give promises of special training in particular technical fields, to entice pupils to come. But here Alfred Povlsen intervened sharply and with authority: The High Schools should keep on the right lines and refrain from specializing. In the long run, however, it was impossible to avoid some specialization occurring in the High Schools.

The High School, Folk University and Student Association

Up to the change of political system in 1901, there had been agreement between the radical (European) and moderate (Danish) Left on their political aim: the realisation of parliamentarism. The common struggle for political freedom had naturally involved that the disagreements were less conspicuous. But they manifested themselves all the more clearly, after the change of system, particularly in divergent views of the work of folk enlightenment.

Both the Radical wing, which was represented by the Student Association with Georg Brandes at their head, and the Folk High School courted folk youth. In a speech at the Student Association summer meeting in 1902, Brandes declared that whereas the Folk High Schools were nationally narrow-minded and stood for »belief and the past«, the Student Association's educational work and the education at the Folk University established in 1897 represented »hope and the future«. The education at the High Schools was furtive as regards the results of science, particularly natural science. For the High School folk, truth should correspond with religious conviction.

Alfred Povlsen replied. He believed that one could no longer – if one ever had been able to – accuse the High Schools of narrow nationalism. Nor did they avoid natural science and evolution. In addition, they met each year with men from the university to attend courses of lectures, for example on natural science, and it was the university itself that decided the subjects of the lectures.

Now the representatives of the Folk University joined in the debate, and established that the Student Association's lecture activities had nothing to do with Folk University education. But at the same time they pointed out the differences between the aims of the Folk High School and the Folk University educa-

Krogerup High School. Bird's-eye view of the campus.

Krogerup High School, with the old main building, built in 1779.

Ollerup Gymnastics High School.

Egmont High School, which is specially equipped for handicapped students.

The Jutland Physical Training School, Vejle.

Creative activities out-of-doors at Rødding High School.

tional activity: »The Folk High School does not only aim at enlarging its pupils' horizon and giving them knowledge, its aim is also through teaching to work for a particular Christian belief. The latter is remote from the Folk University programme.« It was also the Folk University men's opinion that the Student Association like the Folk High School aimed at more than »to make the results and methods of science known to wider circles«. They both worked for the spread of a particular view of life.

There were thus three directions in the work of folk enlightenment: the Folk High School, which worked from a Christian basic view, the Student Association's lecture activity, which built upon the Brandes view of life, and the Folk University, which was neutral as to religion.

Circles unfamiliar with the High Schools

In the non-farming strata of the population – now large – it was still difficult for the Folk High School to get a footing. But as a new development, in 1905, the Copenhagen stationer Louis Petersen's widow, Mrs. Ludi Petersen, started a small Folk High School, The Merchants' Rest, in Hørsholm, for young shop assistants. In 1908 a High School was founded for fishermen, in rented rooms in Kerteminde. Later they obtained their own building in Snoghøj, by the Little Belt. But after some years the school was turned into a girls' Gymnastics High School because of lack of pupils.

The Copenhagen day high school, Borup's High School, on the other hand, continued to grow. In 1919/20 the attendance was 700.

In 1910, on Social Democratic initiative, Esbjerg Workers High School was started. The men who led this work were the Chairman of the Social Democratic Electoral Association, the editor J. P. Sundbo, and the secondary school teacher Jørgen Banke. They were both former High School pupils. Sundbo had great plans. He visualized establishing a number of high schools, which were to be centres of spiritual energy for the working classes, just as the traditional High Schools had been

e Travelling High School. The windmill at Tvind for alternative energy,
lt by the teachers aided by outside labour.

for the farming classes. The High School in Esbjerg was to be the first. Banke wanted a school modelled on the Swedish Folk High School in Brunnsvik, to give more meaning to the leisure hours of young people in the towns. They rented rooms for a day high school in the Esbjerg Technical School. There were five-months winter terms from November to April. In his speech at the opening on 3 November 1910, Sundbo stressed that although this Workers' High School had a socialistic view of life, it was not a school for Socialist agitators. The main subjects were the natural sciences, civics, and history beginning with the French Revolution. Alone among the High Schools of the time, Esbjerg Workers High School had no religious morning service, and instead of the High School Song Book, with all its national songs, the Workers' Song Book was used. This did contain revolutionary songs, but these were omitted from the later editions of the song book, and replaced by hiking songs and ballads, often translated from German.

In 1917, Esbjerg Workers High School was able to move into its own school building, which had rooms for 100 pupils, and in 1919/20 all were filled.

In order to establish contact with the circles in the towns which were not familiar with the High Schools, Askov High School's Board of Directors decided to expand the High School extension still further. The State subsidy was doubled, so that more teachers could be engaged, and new subjects were included in the time table such as historical biology, civics and comparative religion.

In 1914, on the same premises that a High School was needed which could unite the country and the towns, the Left wing Liberal party men Tormod Jørgensen and Ejnar Munk together opened an extension to Høng High School, where Grundtvig's idea for Sorø school was tested and maintained (but not as a State High School). It had a highly qualified teaching staff, amongst them a man with experience of the Social Democratic educational work, but the school was run on modest lines. After the experiment with the extension to the High School had been tried for 11 years, they had to give up, and the school was changed into a small-holders school.

82

The High Schools during the First World War

As mentioned earlier, the numbers of pupils fell after the outbreak of war. This was due partly to the exceptional call-up for the Defence Forces, and partly to the absence of young men from the Danish-minded but German North Slesvig. As German citizens they had to go to the Front and fight for a cause which was not theirs. As a gift to the prison camps in the warring countries, and an encouragement to folk enlightenment work among the prisoners of war, the Association of High Schools and Agricultural Schools published a book on the High Schools. This was translated into English, German, French and Russian.

By a cautious policy of neutrality Denmark succeeded in keeping out of the Great Powers' war. Throughout the High School world the War was regarded as the greatest human catastrophe. But it caused a sensation when Alfred Povlsen, who had previously dissociated himself from Hørup's »total disarmament«, now went in for brotherhood between nations and international co-operation. His views became something of a programme for large circles in the Danish High Schools in the period which followed.

But the cause nearest the hearts of the High School men was the return of the Danish-minded North Slesvig to Denmark. Leaders of the national struggle south of the frontier had been recruited during the years from the High Schools. They returned to their home districts and obtained leading positions in cultural work. The most important of these was Hans Peter Hanssen Nørremølle, who was from an old family of farmers in the Åbenrå area. He had been to Askov High School for three winters, had followed German politics in Berlin, and had attended lectures at Leipzig University. He was therefore equipped with a wide range of knowledge, and was in possession of a historical and comprehensive political view. In the years 1896–1908 he was a member of the Prussian Diet, and in 1908–1919 of the German Parliament.

During the attempt in the German Empire to bring about a change of political system in October 1918, he made the demand, in the German Parliament, that the North Slesvig question be solved in accordance with § 5 in the Prague Peace of 1866 between Prussia and Austria, which had been cancelled unilaterally by the Germans after the war with France in 1871. This contained a promise according to which the northern districts of Slesvig would be returned to Denmark, if the population expressed a wish for it, in a free plebiscite. Further he claimed the same rights for the German-minded inhabitants north of the coming frontier as for the Danish minority south of this frontier. The great majority of High School men went in for H. P. Hanssen Nørremølle's line of thought, where the principle of self-determination should be brought into use during the preparations for the return of North Slesvig to Denmark. In accordance with this, the frontier was finally drawn north of Flensborg. The Allied Governments were notified of this on 15 June 1920, and on the day of reunion, 10 June, King Christian X rode across the old frontier. He finished his tour into the reunited land with a visit to Askov High School.

The course of the frontier was a great disappointment to the »Flensborg folk«, as they were called, who wanted Flensborg returned to Denmark, in spite of its German majority.

VI.

THE INTERWAR PERIOD AND THE SECOND WORLD WAR

Unsettled Times

The years 1920–1945 wiped out many boundary lines. The tension between population strata diminished. The expression »the common people« became a thing of the past. And like the social barriers, the cultural barriers, too, were broken down. Everyone read the same newspapers, went to the same cinemas and theatres, and listened to the same radio broadcasts. But it was a winding path that led to the principle of democratic equality. Hope and fear alternated in the years up to the end of the Second World War.

The twenties have been called the years of optimism. American businessmen and economists prophesied a golden age, without crises, and with constant progress. Unflagging optimism also spread to Denmark. Highflown expectations were entertained of peace and of the newly established League of Nations. It was the older generation that was responsible for the War. The trenches at Verdun had exposed them. Now the younger generation would join in building up a freer, more sensible and happier era.

But after the carefree progress of the twenties, and the gay parties, came the morning after. The great crash on the New York Stock Exchange in the autumn 1929 started a grave economic crisis in the U.S.A., and during 1930 this spread to Europe, where practically every country and every trade was hit.

In Denmark the crisis foreshadowed a decade of poverty and fear, with threats from the south, where Hitler seized power. Factories and businesses had to close. Unemployment reached an average of 24% in the years 1932–1938. Farming was also badly hit: interest on capital investment was negative in 1931–32, and there was little improvement in the next few years. Many farms were sold up. In addition, a semi-Nazi farmers' movement created political unrest. However, a large meeting was held in Odense in 1934, where High School folk protested strongly and with authority at the attacks on the democratic way of life. The High Schools did not see it as their job to take lessons from the German Nazi movement.

The total intake of pupils at the High Schools was less in the thirties than in the twenties, for one reason because the drop in farm workers' wages was not followed up by a parallel fall in the fees to be paid by pupils. A term at High School became too expensive. Young unemployed persons could, certainly, have their High School term paid for by the public authorities, so that more pupils from the towns attended High School in those years, but this could not balance the decrease in pupils from traditional High School circles:

	1920/21	1925/26	1930/31	1935/36	1940/41	1944/45
Number of High Schools	58	59	59	59	54	54
Number of pupils	7006	6719	6407	6366	6023	6049
High School frequency	13%	11%	10%	10%	9%	9%

During these years, 16 new High Schools were started, whilst 20 High Schools were closed or converted to other uses, such as preliminary schools for hospital nurses, agricultural schools, small-holders schools, continuation schools for 14 to 18-year-olds, etc. As in the years before 1920, it was the small local schools which were the hardest hit.

The Grundtvig High Schools had never been purely informative schools. Nor did they change their character after 1920. But now, greater importance was attached technical education, as compared with life enlightenment. At the same time, changes occurred in the form and content of the teaching. Lectures had to give pláce to some extent to the study groups which gave the young people the opportunity for independent work. New subjects were taken up: modern history instead of ancient history, Europe and distant continents instead of the history of the North. The Folk High School gave inspiration and impulse in a very different area from its previous sphere.

Southern Jutland

Interest in the struggle for the national frontier faded somewhat into the background after the return of North Slesvig to Denmark in 1920. Again and again, when one of the Folk High School aims was achieved, a crisis followed. This had been the case when, thanks to the Co-operative Movement, the peasant classes had achieved economic and social equality with other social classes; when in 1901 farmers had obtained seats on the King's Council; when Christen Kold's pupils had succeeded in getting the democratic June Constitution carried through in 1915; and not least now, when the North Slesvigians had been reunited with Denmark. The older High School folk felt that they seemed to have lost some of the inspiration and the purpose of their work.

But there were others for whom the very transition from German to Danish after 56 years of foreign rule presented considerable problems. Developments had taken place in Denmark in which the Southern Jutlanders had had little or no part: the reorganisation of agriculture, with all the co-operative undertakings and the export to England, as well as all the industrialization which had been carried out, not to mention the developments in the parliamentary system in Denmark, and cultural developments. It was only through the High Schools that the Southern Jutlanders had had personal contact with Denmark.

It was therefore natural that High Schools were also started in South Jutland after the Reunion. In November 1920, Rødding High School was reopened. On Als, Danebod High School was started, and later a High School in Rønshoved on Flensborg Fjord, while the Home Mission acquired a High School in Hoptrup, between Haderslev and Åbenrå.

After 1864, Cornelius Appel, Ludvig Schrøder's successor, had been deprived of the right to carry High School activity for male students in Rødding. Up to 1889 he was able to keep the school running for girls. In 1920, his son, Jacob Appel, as Minister of Education for the German minority, carried through a settlement which had been refused the Danish South Jutlanders under foreign rule. In the towns, the Folk High Schools received German-language departments, and in the country German primary schools could be established if 20% of the electors, representing at least 10 children, applied for it. In addition, the German minority could start private schools with the same rules for State grants as the Grundtvigian Free Schools. The appointment of teachers need not be confirmed by the Danish authorities, and the schools were not subject to Danish inspection.

Such far-reaching consideration for a national minority has hardly been seen anywhere else in the world. In March 1933, the German primary schools obtained independent parent committees, as did the private schools. They had the exclusive right of decision on the appointment of teachers and the choice of textbooks. This meant purely German autonomy as regards their schools. At the same time, no one could foresee that this broad-minded school system, for which the High School men, true to Grundtvig's ideas, were mainly responsible, would later be so grossly exploited by the National Socialist Germans.

The interwar years were hard for those farmers who had bought their farms before 1920. The German *mark* lost its value in relation to the Danish *krone*. This depreciation meant that farmers in South Jutland had not sufficient capital to survive the agricultural crisis at the beginning of the thirties. Five times as many farms had to be sold up here as in the rest of Denmark, north of the King's River. Many maintained that farming conditions had been better under the German regime. It was a period of tension caused by the economic and frontier problems.

On the Danish side, the High School man Hans Lund stood in the front line in the »second fight for South Jutland«. That January day in 1933, when Hitler became Reich Chancellor, Lund's gloomy words were heard in Rødding High School: »Now the N. C. O. rules in Germany, Goethe's land«. From the first he was an enemy of Nazism and extraparliamentary activity. But both in the national and the political struggle he would only make use of democratic means.

The Pioneers

In the first interwar years, a number of High Schools were still marked by an introspective view of life. Holger Begtrup was aware of its weakness. In his lecture at Askov High School's 60 years jubilee in 1925, he said in part:

».. . But I must admit that the Folk High School suffers from one great lack, in our days. It has narrowed down its spiritual activity all too much, to enlightenment for life in the individual soul and home circles. It has become, so to speak, too private, and has no living relationship to the country at large nor to the great questions of mankind's world around us, as the old High Schools had in relation to the opportunities of their times.«

In one sense, Begtrup's words were spoken *post festum*. A new generation was taking over in those years. There were new men on the captain's bridge. The interwar years were rich in clear-cut personalities within the High School world. Alfred Povlsen had put forward the ideas of world citizenship during the War, and these inspired prominent High School folk of the younger generation, amongst them, four Askov teachers, known as »the fourleaf clover« (after Grundtvig's High School pamphlet of the same name). It consisted of the historian Hans Lund, the natural science teachers J. Th. Arnfred and Jens Rosenkjær, and the historian C. P. O. Christiansen. In 1921 they started the »Danish Outlook«, which became one of Denmark's leading cultural periodicals, and which showed that they had a keen eye for the global challenges of the times. In 1971 the periodical celebrated its 50 years jubilee.

89

Like Hans Lund, J. Th. Arnfred was the son of a farmer from West Jutland. He was deeply rooted in folk culture, and had a watchful eye for all the new ideas which were stirring at the time. He came to Askov as a teacher in 1910. In 1928 he succeeded Jacob Appel, and was principal until 1953. In 1932 he took the initiative in starting *The Nordic Teachers Course,* which ran parallel to the school's normal summer school. For a number of years Arnfred was also Chairman of the Association of High Schools and Agricultural Schools, and it was he who more than all others represented the High Schools *vis-à-vis* the outside world. His democratic negotiating abilities and his skill in mediating between opponents were very useful in his work in the Co-operative Movement, where he had a leading position. By profession Arnfred was a civil engineer, but his field of interest was far wider than the mathematical natural scientific line, ranging from psychology to the study of Christianity, with incursions into the spheres of sociology and political economy.

Jens Rosenkjær was a teacher at Askov High School in 1911–1925. His subject was historical chemistry, later also historical biology. The subject of biology had previously been neglected, when the theory of evolution, and Darwinism, were dangerous words, but now teachers were to speak plainly with the pupils on modern scientific views. As a teacher, Rosenkjær was able to make the most difficult material accessible to everyone, from the student to the simplest village girl. From biology his interests led him to international political subjects.

C. P. O. Christiansen was a teacher at Askov High School in 1913–1934, and afterwards principal of Frederiksborg (Grundtvig's) High School until 1951. Like Hans Lund he became a historian in the service of the High School.

His idea, that individual folk and folk groups each had their purpose, led him to the so-called »new Nordic« outlook. This did not, however, have any greater Scandinavia in view. The individual Nordic nations should preserve their freedom and independence, and folk life and language. Only through co-operation between them, in a Nordic federal state – not by their amalgamation in a federation – could the new Nordic idea be realised and a new strong North arise.

In 1921, Peter Manniche started the International High School in Helsingør (Elsinore), and was its principal until 1954. He had conceived the idea in England during the War, and it had met with sympathetic response among the Quakers and in university circles. Manniche succeeded in getting English, German and American teachers attached to the school, and the numbers of pupils grew steadily from year to year. His idea of a school for world citizenship, regardless of all national frontiers, aroused interest all over the world.

This global orientation allied itself with pacifist currents coming to Denmark from abroad. At all international congresses, resolutions were passed for world peace and against war. In Denmark, a university professor called national feeling a form of disease, which would surely disappear altogether. The Social Democrat Ministers demanded disarmament. But it would be unjust to assert that the anti-militaristic feeling of the interwar period was simply an expression of inanity and dull materialism. Many of the High Schools' best pupils wore the emblem of the conscientious objectors in their buttonholes – broken guns. A pacifist wing of High School folk had the most out-of-date war songs from the events of 1848 and 1864, omitted from the High School Song Book in the edition published in 1926. The idyl prevailing in interwar Denmark was not noticeably disturbed, even by the signs of unrest in the south after Hitler seized power.

In 1931, The Nordic Folk High School in Geneva was founded, to hold a course every summer for participants from Denmark, Norway, Finland and Sweden. Its object was to supply information on international and Nordic problems, in High School conditions. The main emphasis was later laid on the activities carried on by the International Labour Organisation (the ILO), the World Health Organisation (WHO) and UNESCO. The school was open to all, but addressed itself especially to persons in organisations or other activities, who would take active part in international work in and outside the North. It was run by an association which numbered the Nordic

Labour Information Organisations among its members. Among the leaders of these courses, which usually began in May, there have been High School men from the Nordic countries. Part of the course was transferred to Geneva, where there was opportunity to follow the proceedings of the General Assembly and the ILO. After the War, the course finished with a week in France with visits to UNESCO and the OECD.

The Humanist Outlook

Some of the most important representatives of the Folk High School between the wars allied themselves to the humanist trends.

As a young man, Uffe Grosen, who was Principal of Vallekilde High School in 1923–1954, encouraged by Begtrup, had spent a term at the British Quaker School, Woodbrook. In the years 1910–1912 Begtrup had established contact with the Quaker schools, and when he returned he declared: »We will put in a window to the West in our schoolroom.« This was also what Grosen wanted. During several visits to England he was influenced not only by the British way of thought and life in general, but by the Quakers' attitude to war and violent methods. Gandhi also meant a great deal to him. His Social Liberal basic views were close to those of Begtrup and Bredsdorff. Throughout, he stood four-square on the Grundtvigian Folk High School's Christian folk foundation, to which his many carefully prepared lectures bear witness. Under his leadership, Vallekilde High School flourished again.

Johannes Novrup was a teacher at the International High School in 1928–1931, and at Askov High School in 1931–1942. Like so many other students at Copenhagen University in the 1920's, he was strongly influenced by the religious historian Vilhelm Grønbech. But what stirred his pupils most was the spirit which animated him – the spirit which the missionary Albert Schweitzer called »reverence for life«. Novrup was a personal friend of Albert Schweitzer, whose books he had translated into Danish. In his own books, which dealt with the problems of adult education, he represented the High School in the interwar period, to the outside world. It was especially such characteristics as tolerance and humanity that he particularly valued, but he could be intolerant, even passionate, on the subject of opinions and ideas which vulgarized and tabulated life. All adult education should be carried out under mutual obligation, in an atmosphere of freedom and confidence. The teacher, he said, »should come down from the rostrum and be a human being among human beings«. For this reason, study groups and conversation were essential to his teaching.

The humanist wing was strongly attacked by the so-called »mythologists«, whose most influential representative was Åge Møller, Principal of Rønshoved High School in 1921–1941. He found that the interwar High School had failed. It had simply been an informative school, which gave too much factual orientation (often with the Statistical Year Book as a manual!) and popularized the findings of science. He was convinced that the proper High School material was to be found in the myths, the Nordic bible of folk life, which contained the experience of the ancients in the basic conditions of life in every age. For a time he had a considerable following among the young High School folk.

The Workers' Educational Association's High School Activity

In 1924, the Workers' Educational Association (AOF) was started, on the lines of the *Arbetarnes Bildningsförbund* in Sweden. It was a Social Democratic body, which organised its work of information in evening classes. In addition it published the study circles' books on civics, trade union information, co-operation, community information, political history, educational questions, etc.

In 1930 the AOF took over both Esbjerg High School and Roskilde High School. According to their charter, the Workers High Schools' purpose was to inform young workers and other pupils from town and country, give them an all-round education, and hold short courses for the members of the Social

Democratic Labour Movement, their collaborators and shop stewards.

During the depression at the beginning of the 1930's, the Workers High Schools were attended by long-term unemployed, who had long since used up their right to assistance. If they went to High School, they could have the whole term paid for by the public authorities, as well as a little pocket money, and of two evils they chose the lesser, even though it was not a semester at a High School they were wanting, but work. Having unemployed at the ordinary High Schools had not been a success. They felt bitter against a society which treated them as step-children. They could not work in the team with farmers' sons, who had saved up for their High School terms themselves, and who came there with the self-esteem which belonged to »the mainstays of society«. In farming circles it was generally believed that a High School attended by many unemployed was not an institution to which one could entrust one's young people. It was better at the Workers High Schools, where the disparity between urban workers and farm workers from the country did not exist.

In the educational work for the unemployed, Hjalmar Gammelgård became particularly influential. He was Principal of Roskilde High School in 1930–35. He grew up in a home strongly influenced by Christen Kold's Christian outlook, but later, in the atheistic Student Union, he became absorbed by the Brandesian educational ideas. He did not regard his High School work as a John the Baptist calling, and declared that the Folk High School should not preach a definite outlook on life, either religious or political, but should bring problems up to debate. It should give humanity, vision, and a broad outlook, and awaken a desire for experience.

High Schools with Technical Departments, and Technical High Schools

Whilst in the old days, many High Schools had had an agricultural department, an artisan department, a domestic science department, a gymnastics department, or other special department, Technical High Schools were a novelty which came into being in the interwar period. The dividing line between these two school forms was undefined. But the Technical High Schools, particularly, met a need for an education with a more or less commercial purpose.

Among the Technical High Schools which were started in these years were 5 nursing preparatory schools, a male nurses high school, a high school for co-operative stores assistants, and a high school for child welfare institution assistants. It was a condition for State aid that the pupils also took part in general educational classes, and the Technical High Schools were not allowed to prepare for examinations. However, dispensation was given to certain schools which prepared pupils for teachers' colleges.

The training of gymnastics instructors had no professional aim. It was meant for the training of leaders of the voluntary men's and women's gymnastics, abjuring individual performance and equilibristic acts, at the expense of exercises in which everyone could take part. Had it not been for the leaders' training in gymnastics, a term at a High School, from which the pupils simply returned to their previous work, could hardly have attracted so many of the farming youth during the years of agricultural crisis after 1930. They undertook the organisation and instruction of gymnastics in the local youth clubs on a voluntary basis, and were often elected to the boards of directors. They became the link between the High Schools and their home districts.

The Gymnastics High Schools were the culmination of this folk gymnastics work. A start was made when Niels Bukh, who had led a gymnastics department at Ollerup High School, opened his own Gymnastics High School in 1920. In 1925, two women gymnastics teachers Jørgine Abildgaard and Anna Krog, bought the former Fishermen's High School in Snoghøj, and equipped it as a Gymnastics High School for Women, and in 1938 the Physical Training High School in Gerlev was started. The Gymnastics High Schools were well attended.

In answer to the supporters of the »pure« High School, the staffs of the Technical High Schools claimed that Technical

High Schools were attracting numbers of pupils from circles unfamiliar with the Folk High Schools. In addition, they declared that many young people of about 20 years of age felt it unnatural to study intellectual subjects, such as history, art appreciation, literature etc., from morning to night. They were not happy without practical utilitarian teaching and physical exercise! »It is not good for one's digestion to eat only white bread,« one of the technical school supporters wrote. »One must also chew coarse rye bread. The High Schools must have some rye bread subjects in between.«

From the other side it was pointed out that the practical, utilitarian subjects, and the subjects with a purely commercial intention at the Technical High Schools took up much of the pupils' energy and attention. It was particularly unfortunate if the all-round educational subjects were pushed into the background altogether, or if the technical subjects were camouflaged as High School subjects. The spacious High School Act often left too much to the discretion of the principal.

The Occupation

On 9 April 1940, Denmark was occupied by German troops. This took place without much military resistance, but under protest. The King and the Government called for discipline and order. The black-out followed, and then censorship of the radio and the press. On the other hand, the Germans gave an official promise that they would respect Denmark's territorial and political integrity.

The population was deeply divided. There were schools which laid the main responsibility for the catastrophe upon the 1930's Social Democratic and pacifist policy. Anti-parliamentary, Nazi-inspired »regeneration groups« went even further, and attacked »the system«. They demanded new men at the helm, without respect to the opinions of the electorate. In June, in recognition of this danger, *The Elders' Council* was set up, consisting of men whose roots were in the Folk High School and Grundtvig circles. Their object was to organise support for pas-

Assembly Hall at Krogerup High School.

Herning High School Library.

Interior from Odder High School.

Lecture Hall at Støvring High School.

Pupils' room at Rødding High School.

The Family High School, Skærgården, where students may bring their children. Student room.

sive resistance against German Nazi influence, by efforts towards national and cultural unity, on a democratic basis. They established contact with the leaders of the political youth organisations which were co-ordinated in the *Danish Youth Association*. This was to »encourage the will of youth for Danish character and sense of responsibility towards the mother country, strengthen solidarity and create respect for Denmark's history and past, and trust in Denmark's future«.

A veritable »Grundtvig wave« swept over the country. It reached its first climax in the autumn 1940, when Hal Koch held a series of lectures at Copenhagen University. The attendance was enormous. Hal Koch, who was 36 at the time, was professor in church history. Up to that time, he had devoted himself to science, and had taken no part in the current debate, but now he felt that the time had come to strike a blow for democracy. In one of the many lectures which he held, he took his stand in the centre of events when he gave a warning against the »regenerators«: »I shall not speak on politics, but I warn you against letting yourselves be carried away by the tremendous fellows who have now appeared, who can all hold judgement day on our past.« Hal Koch was afraid that the widespread national feeling might end in Danish Nazism. He was elected Chairman of the Danish Youth Association, and in his declaration of intent he laid down that the purpose of the Danish Youth Association should be a deliberate effort to make youth politically aware by lectures and study circles – the only effective reply to Nazi propaganda. It was first of all thanks to him that a democratic point of view came to ride the crest of the waves from national revival.

In the winter 1940–41, democracy seemed already to have survived the crisis. Folk meetings, evening classes and High Schools were attended as never before. With the support of all the political parties, the Minister of Education Jørgen Jørgensen, who was a member of The Elders' Council and himself a former High School pupil, prepared a new law on Folk High Schools, which came into force on 4 July 1942. This not only gave aid to needy High School pupils, it also gave far-reaching support for teachers' salaries and maintenance of school build-

ev High School. Two generations meet.

ings, and loans on favourable conditions to the High Schools, which became self-governing institutions.

The Election of 23 March 1943 was a great victory for Hal Koch and the Danish Youth Association's coalition policy. The voting percentage was 89.5, the largest in the history of the country. The anti-parliamentary parties suffered a stinging defeat.

But now, a new front made its appearance: the Resistance Movement. There were also Danes who organised active resistance against the Occupying Power, with illegal newspapers, sabotage of important military railway transport, and of factories delivering goods of importance to the German prosecution of the war. A condition for this was close co-operation with the British Special Operations Executive (SOE), for example in dropping operations of SOE parachutists, arms and sabotage materiel. The first unofficial information contact with Great Britain was started as early as the autumn 1940, when *Berlingske Tidende*'s foreign correspondent in Stockholm, Ebbe Munck (later Lord Chamberlain) established himself as the central pivot of Danish intelligence – and later of Resistance matters in general – between the Danes and the British. Well-known Resistance men (among them Mogens Fog, Erling Foss, Eigil Borch-Johansen) took on the dangerous work of courier to and from Stockholm. Borch-Johansen, particularly, made many of these journeys. As business manager of the Danish Coastal Shipowners Association, he was well informed on shipping movements in Danish waters, which he passed on to the Intelligence Office in Stockholm. He gradually became deeply involved in illegal activity, with its many ramifications – as did so many Danes, as the months passed. After the German invasion of Russia on 22 June 1941, the Communists also joined the Resistance, which gradually became a national movement. In August 1943, *Denmark's Freedom Council* was formed.

Hal Koch dissociated himself from the illegal activities of the Resistance Movement, with its purpose of bringing Denmark over on to the side of the Allies in the war with Germany. On 28 August 1943 came the break with the German Occupation Authorities. The Government ceased to function. Martial law was proclaimed. The Germans took over the administrative authority, with summary courts and the death penalty for sabotage. Arrests and terror increased from month to month. But now, the Resistance Movement had become a nation-wide movement, and before Germany capitulated on 4 May 1945, it had seen to it that it should have as many members in the Liberation Government as the coalition parties.

In the autumn 1944, the Danish Folk High School could celebrate a modest centenary. The German Occupation Authorities had not prevented the High Schools' cultural work or their ardent defence of Danish democracy. On the other hand, more and more of the High Schools were hit by troublesome requisitioning. They had to transfer their activities to seaside hotels, manors and large farms, and the pupils had to share large dormitories.

As humanists, many High School men found it difficult to adjust themselves to the Resistance Movement's struggle, with violent methods. Others became fine examples for youth, by both fighting Nazi activity and carrying out practical humanitarian work for the many thousands of German refugees from East Prussia, West Prussia and Pomerania, who streamed into Denmark in the last months of the War.

VII.

THE POSTWAR PERIOD

Changes in the Structure of Society

Denmark in Transformation was the title of a much discussed book, published in the 1960's by Denmark's Radio. The title itself is symptomatic of the whole complex of problems in the postwar period. In these years, Denmark has been through an industrialization which is just as sweeping as the industrial revolution in England, 150–200 years ago. In the first postwar years, agriculture was still the most important source of export, but in the years from 1958 to 1973, industry's share of the country's total export value rose from 39% to 52%. The migration from agriculture, the High Schools' most important recruiting field, rose increasingly. The number of young farm workers fell from year to year. In 1950, there were 200,000 permanent farm workers in agriculture. In 1975 only 27,000. In 1950, the farming community constituted 21% of the whole population. In 1975 only 7%. More than one-third of the independent farms disappeared in amalgamations and discontinuation. The farms became one-man agricultural factories. It was the small-holders who were the hardest hit. As a result of this development, 5 Small-holders High Schools, which were approved as Agricultural Schools but were something between agricultural and high schools, had to close or transfer to other activities. The number of Agricultural Schools also fell. By an Act of Parliament in 1970, they were subjected to closer direction by public authorities.

On the other hand, the population in the towns and urban built-up areas grew in the postwar years by 50–60%, particularly in residential developments. But many new investments caused pollution, and following labour-saving technological rationalization, the total personnel engaged in industry did not increase, and from 1970 showed a tendency to fall. However, considerable manpower was absorbed in the service areas, particularly within the public sector (administration, police, defence, education, social and health services). After the oil crisis in 1973, unemployment followed.

The following table shows the division of employment in percentages, in 1950–1975:

	1950	*1960*	*1970*	*1975*
Agriculture, fisheries, etc	26	18	11	9
Manufacture, etc.,				
building and construction	34	37	38	34
Trade and transport	20	21	22	22
Services, professional				
activity, etc	18	21	26	33
Unspecified	2	3	3	2
	100%	100%	100%	100%

It should be added, as regards these statistics, that in 1975 fisheries represented 2% of the agriculture and fisheries percentage of 9%. The percentage of trade and transport showed only a slight increase.

The gradual reduction of customs barriers placed Denmark among the countries of the world with the highest standard of living. With the rise in wealth and the welfare state, an increasing desire to rise in the social scale appeared in wide sectors of the population. This was apparent from the frequency of Matriculation Examinations alone (the yearly number of young people who finished their schooling with a »student examination« in relation to a year of 19-year-olds as a whole). This frequency was 3% in 1940, and 18% in 1975. Added to this considerable increase in the number of university students, there was a large number of young people who passed the newly started *Higher Preparatory Examination* in 1970. In 1978, 28.5% of the young people of that year went to upper secondary school.

Educational Reforms and the Folk High School

The most important reform was the Act of 1958 on the *Folkeskole* (the Primary and Lower Secondary School), by which the middle school examination was replaced by State-controlled tests after 8th, 9th, and later the 10th school years. At the same time, a 3-year secondary school with a final examination was introduced as a permanency. The result was that the number of pupils who had attended the 8th and 9th forms in the course of the 60's rose to 90%, and the frequency of the secondary school final examination (the secondary school examinations in relation to the total number of 17-year-olds) rose from 15% in 1950 to 40% in 1975.

With the Primary and Lower Secondary School Act of 1975, the secondary school examination was abolished, with the tests and examinations in the primary schools up to that time. The state-controlled tests after the 9th form and the Technical Preparatory Examination were held for the last time in 1977, whilst the state-controlled tests after the 10th form, the Extended Technical Preparatory Examination and the Secondary School Examination were held for the last time in 1978. From 1977 (8th form), 1978 (9th form) and 1979 (10th form) the *Primary School's Final Test* (which can be taken in 11 subjects), and the *Primary School's Extended Final Test* which can be taken in 5 subjects after the 10th form, and corresponds approximately to the Secondary School Examination, were introduced.

With the new system of tests there was no question, however, of any overall test or examination, but of final tests in each subject. The pupils themselves decide whether they will present themselves for the test in the individual subject, and there is no criterion for a pass, either in the overall result or in connexion with the subject in question.

The introduction of the Higher Preparatory Examination (HF) was another important reform. It was held first in 1969, at the same time as the new Teacher Training Act came into force. The Higher Preparatory Examination now permits matriculation at all advanced educational institutions, on an equal footing with the »student examination« (the final examination at an upper secondary school), but it is characterized by greater freedom of choice. The examination can be held at the same time in all or several subjects, or tests can be held in one subject at a time. To enroll for a course for the Higher Preparatory Examination, no preliminary examination and schooling is required, if the necessary preparatory knowledge has been acquired in some other way. For a time, several High Schools held preparatory courses, particularly in mathematics and languages, for those who wished to matriculate. *The State Education Aid,* for students of 18 years and over, was an important condition for the extended use of the educational offers. Thus all those qualified to study were able to get their necessary expenses met through subsidies and cheap loans.

Even though the educational explosion also left its mark on the High Schools, the latter insisted that they wished to stand aloof from the official educational system. It turned out that, in spite of competition from the business training schools, and the establishment of many new upper secondary schools, they had been able to maintain their intake of 18 to 25-year-olds. The recruitment of pupils from among the many unemployed young people, from the middle of the 1970's, contributed considerably to this.

The increasing quantity of educational offers altered the High Schools' significance for democracy. When the new Constitution was passed in 1953, 48 of the 179 Members of Parliament elected in a General Election the same year had been at a High School. In 1977, only 22 were former High School pupils, while 77 had taken their »student examination«. This was undoubtedly connected with the decrease in the importance of agriculture as regards employment. In 1953, 29 Members of Parliament had been to an agricultural college; in 1977 only 22.

High School Pupils at the Long Courses

In order to compare the numbers of pupils for the years 1945/46–1977/78 with the numbers for earlier years, the following table includes only the numbers of pupils attending long courses (over 5 weeks' duration):

Numbers of High Schools and Pupils

	Number High Schools	Number Pupils in all	Drawn from Denmark	Proportion of Women Pupils	Number »Year's Pupils«[1]
1945/46	54	4766	4718	48%	
1950/51	58	5866	5590	63%	2434
1955/56	59	6061	5733	66%	2652
1960/61	64	7309	6907	64%	3240
1965/66	69	8732	8230	67%	4140
1970/71	67	9030	8270	63%	4141
1975/76	83	9764	9083	60%	4339
1976/77	83	9483	8885	57%	4162
1t77/78	84	9846	9189[2]	58%	4444

1. A »year's pupil« is a pupil for 40 weeks. It is an artificial term, used as the basis for calculating State aid since the law regarding aid of 1969 and the High School Act of 1970. The total number of pupils per year is arrived at by multiplying the weekly number by the number of »pupil weeks« and dividing by 40.
2. Of these 328 were from Greenland and 75 from the Faroe Islands.

From 1950/51 to 1977/78, there was a net increase of approved High Schools of 45%. Their average intakes in the years in question were 42 and 50 »year's pupils« respectively.

Number of Foreign Pupils, Classified as to Nationality

	1945/46	1950/51	1955/56	1960/61	1965/66	1970/71	1975/76	1976/77	1977/.
S.Slesvig	15	94	43	35	42	29	20	14	3
Iceland	–	3	35	20	56	26	26	24	4
Norway	25	53	56	94	156	191	169	142	13
Sweden	3	32	31	39	39	61	36	53	5
Rest Europe					–	163	145	163	17
Africa					29	20	31	30	2
Asia	5	94	163	214	15	96	96	62	8
N.America					59	140	z15	92	8
Other countries					106	34	43	18	2
In all	48	276	328	402	502	760	681	598	6.
Share, total number pupils	1%	5%	5%	6%	6%	8%	7%	6%	7%

104

Before the War the intake of foreign pupils at the High Schools was only 150–200.

From about the middle of the 1970's, the High Schools were attended by comparatively more older pupils. This is evident from the following table:

Age Grouping at the Long Courses

	1945/46	1960/61	1970/71	1975/76	1976/77	1977/78
Ages of pupils:						
17 years and under	3%	4%	2%	1%	–	–
18–20 years ....⎱			66%	42%	35%	34%
21–24 years ....⎰	82%	87%	22%	35%	39%	38%
25 years and over	15%	9%	10%	22%	26%	28%
In all	100%	100%	100%	100%	100%	100%

While up to 1970/71 High School pupils' average age was about 20 years, in 1977/78 it reached 24 years.

The structure of the new times was also reflected in the pupils' knowledge. In 1954/55, two-thirds of the pupils had only attended village schools for 7 years and nearly half of these schools with only 2–4 classes. Only one-fifth had finished their schooling with an examination. After this, the education explosion started.

Developments during the following period can be seen from the table below:

Pupil Intakes Grouped as to School-leaving Classes

	1965/66	1970/71	1975/76	1977/78
Class 6–7	33%	14%	9%	7%
Class 8–9 and Secondary class 1–2	24%	26%	18%	17%
Class 10	3%	14%	20%	22%
Secondary class 3	33%	38%	29%	26%
Higher Preparatory Course 1–2 .	–	–	4%	6%
Upper secondary class 1–3	7%	8%	16%	22%
Final class unknown			4%	
In all	100%	100%	100%	100%

More and more High School pupils had no experience of practical work. They simply moved from one school bench to another. A completely new situation arose in education, therefore. In addition, the High Schools were attended increasingly by young people from the towns and built-up areas. In 1945/46, approximately 70% of the men had come from farming homes; in 1977/78, 10% at the most. The wider pupil clientele, for which High School folk had worked for so many years, was at last a reality. In the middle of the 1970's, the occupational grouping of the pupils corresponded more closely than ever before to the occupational grouping of the population. The majority no longer came from the country parishes and the gymnastics courses in the village halls. Now, as in Kold's time, many pupils came whose parents had no High School experience, and who had never heard of the great figures of the High School world.

For the peasant youth of earlier times, who had not encountered many outside impressions, their term at the High School was an experience for life. Many of the High School pupils of the 60's and 70's had been to kibbutzim or had been abroad for a considerable time. For them a High School term was more of an interlude. But among them there were also many for whom the grass lawns of the High Schools were greener than any others. And with the increase in specialization, a new need arose for the High Schools, where a dialogue was possible, athwart the narrow confines of a single subject. The Folk High School showed that it had a right to its name.

Now as before, the High Schools formed a framework for close comradeship between teachers, pupils and staff. Through this community life, they aimed at building up human self-respect. The individual did not only learn to see himself as a link in a larger context. He also learned to know himself as a being of intrinsic value, with his special experience and knowledge, and his special way of processing it all, through which he could contribute something fundamental to society.

Psychological deviates and other losers in society also found their way to the High Schools, and with the economic decline after 1974, unemployed youngsters attended, as they had done in the 1930's. The need for the High Schools also manifested itself in the form of Youth High Schools for the 16 to 19-year-olds, and High Schools for pensioners.

Before 1950, most High Schools had courses for men in the winter months, from November to March, and for women from May to July. This fitted in with the traditional days for change of employment (1 November and 1 May) and with seed-time and harvest. Askov was one of the few High Schools which had co-educational courses in the months November-April. Since then, almost all High Schools have introduced co-education and untraditional semester dates, adjusted to the rhythm of the rest of the school system, e.g. from August or September to Christmas, and from January or February to May or June.

The Short Courses

For many High Schools, short courses were not only a new departure in education, but, as with the hiring out of their premises, also an economic safety belt. According to the 1959 Act, a course should be of at least 3 months' duration. But the Minister could use his discretion to approve courses of at least 2 weeks, and include them in the number of teachers' hours for which grants could be made. According to the 1970 Act, courses were permitted of at least 1 week, with 5 continuous days of teaching. It was a condition, however, that some of the school's own teachers took part in the courses.

The number of »year's pupils« attending the short courses is recorded for the following years:

1970/71	272
1975/76	841
1976/77	927
1977/78	1022

The number of »year's pupils« at the short courses in 1970/71 and 1977/78 totalled respectively 6.2% and 23.0% of the High Schools' number of »year's pupils« in all. There is reason to emphasize that the growing interest in the short courses meant that the High Schools obtained a wider field of contact in the whole population. From the brochure issued jointly by the High School Information Office (p. 116) it is evident that the courses were distributed as follows:

	1975/76	1976/77	1977/78	1978/79
Ordinary courses	83	146	142	170
Family courses	26	39	33	22
Pensioners' courses	84	86	141	175
In all	193	271	316	367

In the course of 4 years there was an increase of 90% in the number of short courses which were included in the brochure. The ordinary courses and the family courses (with nurseries for the children) were either courses on a specific subject or mixed High School teaching. The pensioners' courses were prepared especially for senior citizens.

Among the many subjects offered at the short courses were for example: Christianity, Marxism, art appreciation, alternative forms of energy, ecology, religion and politics in the third world, possibilities for development in the developing countries, topical political problems, 20th century music, books and people, the mass media, creative subjects etc., etc. In 1966 at Vallekilde High School an initiative was taken to the first »Jazz at High School« meeting, and in 1978 these meetings were included in the subjects for which grants were made under the High School Act. Other High Schools began to hold courses in rhythmic music/movement, ensemble playing, folk dancing, etc. Normally there were 2 or 3 subjects from which to choose. Often there were groups of subjects of particular interest to parents, such as child psychology, the family and society, the problems of the young, etc. Children between 4 and 14 could stay at the High School for half price.

These courses were arranged in an enjoyable and untraditional way, with the object of bringing renewal and inspiration to the participants.

Teaching

As the background for the High School changed during the postwar years, the form and content of its teaching took new channels. As the result of the extra years of schooling, the need for brushing up elementary knowledge of Danish and arithmetic receded somewhat. The structural alterations in agriculture led to the technical agricultural subjects disappearing altogether from the time table. But teaching of mathematics, physics and chemistry, as well as foreign languages, still played an important part. These practical subjects were needed, for example, for admission to the Higher Preparatory courses.

The sharp dividing-line, which had once existed between the more or less Grundtvigian High Schools and the Home Mission High Schools, which were decreasing in number, faded more and more. Over and above scripture and Bible studies and the practical subjects, the Home Mission High Schools added more subjects of general and cultural interest. As at so many High Schools, a music side was introduced, a social science side, a sports side, etc. Nevertheless, these schools often left a somewhat forbidding impression in non-Mission circles.

The lecture form, surrounded by special reverence, was no longer a central part of High School teaching. Where earlier there had been 2–3 lectures a day, this changed gradually to 2–3 lectures a week, or less. Study groups alternated with discussions, independent study exercises, study excursions, etc. As a rule, some of the hours were obligatory and common to all, but apart from them, the individual pupil had a free choice between many different possible courses. He/she could therefore arrange his/her schedule as he/she needed or desired. But there were variations from one school to another. As in the case of the short summer courses, the study groups reflected the topical questions of the time. Psychology and various aspects of sociology seem particularly to have interested students. Many felt that the treatment of these subjects should make them relevant to contemporary society. There was now more demand for weaving, batik, textile printing, pottery, photography and other types of workshop hobby subjects than there had been earlier among the hardworking farming youth. But amateur theatricals were also given high priority at many High Schools. And a good many High Schools included the history of ideas and the history of art in their syllabus.

Those wanting physical training or sports to be included in the curriculum, with a view to becoming instructors, attended the sports high schools, which received increasing numbers of pupils, as they also offered general High School subjects. New Physical Training High Schools were started in Viborg, Sønderborg, Vejle and Århus. Snoghøj Physical Training High School was turned into a traditional High School, while Køng High School became a Physical Training High School. The success of these Physical Training High Schools can be accounted for by the fact that the young people interested in a High School term could see that there was a definite aim in it all. At all events, these High Schools were not simply boarding schools with glorified 10th forms! Consequently these schools received more students with Matriculation Examination behind them than did the other High Schools. For example, 40% of the women pupils at the Physical Training High School at Viborg in the winter 1977/78 had their »student examinations«.

In the 1970's, country dancing had a renaissance, which was certainly connected with the revival of interest in all forms of folk music. The pleasure of singing from the High School Song Book returned, after some years where it had been criticized. In 1974, the 16th edition was published, cut down from 821 to 497 songs, although a number of songs and verses in foreign languages had been added. The cuts were not universally approved by the older generation in High School circles. As a result, a supplement to the 16th edition had later to be published, containing the favourites among the songs which had been omitted.

True to High School tradition, the teachers had very varying types of education behind them, as can be seen from the following table regarding permanent High School staff:

	1964	1973
Teachers college training	35%	50%
University training	25%	20%
Other training	40%	30%

In the following section, events abroad and at home in the High School world will be mentioned in chronological order:

The South Slesvig Question

Among the currents of thought coming from abroad, which complicated the problems of the High Schools in the first years after the War, was the national unrest in the German part of Slesvig. Here in South Slesvig, which Denmark had ceded in 1864, and which had remained under Germany when North Slesvig was reunited with Denmark in 1920, there was a strong anti-German movement after the collapse of Germany in 1945. There was an enormous influx of pupils into the local Danish schools. New schools were started, even in districts where there were no children from Danish-speaking homes.

In Denmark a South Slesvig movement arose, agitating for South Slesvig to be freed from German sovereignty and separated from the link with Holstein. There were High School folk in this movement who felt that now again they had a cause to fight for. But both official Denmark and the majority of the population were against moving the frontier. In the King's speech to the Danish Parliament on 9 May 1945, the Danish Prime Minister had declared plainly: »The frontier remains unchanged.« The Government did not wish to exploit Germany's weakness. But this did not restore calm to the question. At a meeting on 24 October, the Association of High Schools and Agricultural Schools passed an appeal to the Government, by a large majority:

»The Danish Government is urged to seek England's recognition of the Danish minority in South Slesvig, to promote an administrative separation between

111

South Slesvig and Holstein, if the South Slesvig population themselves wish it, to work for a binding promise to the South Slesvig population of the right, after a period of years, to establish a frontier on the basis of self-determination, and in the meantime to ensure to Danish work full and real freedom – unimpeded by the danger arising from the invasion of refugees.«

A further decision was passed to take up the work of getting a Danish Folk High School built south of Flensburg.

The High Schools' appeal met no response. In a Note of 19 October 1946 the Government stated that it did not intend to put forward any proposal on a change in the national status of South Slesvig.

In spite of their hopes for a shift of the frontier being dashed, many German-speaking young South Slesvigers came to the Danish High Schools, also in the years that followed. The numbers reached their peak in 1947/48 and 1948/49, with 331 and 337 pupils respectively. Interest flagged, gradually, after this. From 1965, there have never been more than 50 South Slesvigers at the Danish High Schools.

Just as the German minority in North Slesvig had its cultural rallying point, Tinglev, north of the frontier (now converted to a Continuation School for 14 to 18-year-olds), so did the Danish minority in South Slesvig acquire its rallying point, in Jarup-lund, just south of the border, where a High School was opened in 1950.

The Effects of the War

In the autumn 1946, Krogerup High School was started with Hal Koch as Principal. This was the result of the valuable all-party co-operation between the youth organisations in the Danish Youth Association.

The fund for Krogerup High School, which started in the main building of an old manor, was contributed by the Employers' Confederation, the Central Co-operative Committee and the Federation of Trade Unions. The teaching staff was highly qualified, including as it did the historian Roar Skovmand and the political economists Poul Nyboe Andersen and K. B. Andersen. The two last-mentioned were later to fill impor-

Kolding High School. Dinner.

The kindergarten at Askov High School.

Lecture Hall at Herning High School.

A class at the Jutland Pensioners High School at Nr. Nissum.

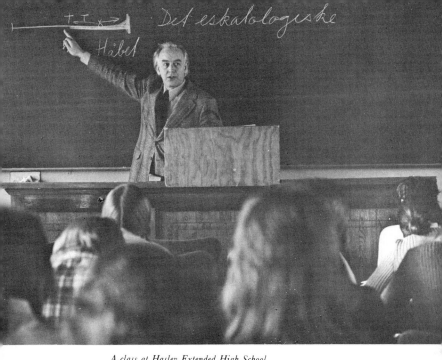

A class at Haslev Extended High School.

Herning High School. Artistic expression.

Haslev High School. Group work.

The Pottery Workshop at Båring High School.

tant ministerial posts in the Liberal and Social Democratic Governments.

The aim of Hal Koch's Citizens School was to strengthen a sense of responsibility, to make the young people politically aware. The idea was not to cultivate any ready-made outlook on life: »The school shall not give the pupils a Christian, national, political or social belief. But it shall, so far as it is in the teachers' power to do so and can be done during the hours of discussion, prevent the pupils from running away from realities.«

The school's objective was to have equal numbers of pupils from the country and the towns. But the rural element, from homes with a High School tradition and the so-called folk circles, failed to come. Nearly all the pupils were from circles unfamiliar with the High School.

In the meantime, Hal Koch's work as Chairman of the Youth Commission, which advocated social reform, brought him into irreconcilable opposition to the representatives of the Farmers and Small-holders Union. In 1956, he retired from the post of Principal. Under the principals who succeeded him, the special character which he gave Krogerup was not maintained.

Johannes Novrup had a great deal in common with Hal Koch, in his view of the aims of the High School. In 1951 he started *Magleås High School* near Birkerød in North Zealand. He received support from the organisation, the *Friends of Peace Relief Fund*. It was later closed.

Båring High School, which was established on a local level and without regard to social barriers, was the result of the comradeship of the years of occupation, as was Krogerup High School, but more on the basis of the Resistance Movement. For economic reasons, however, the plan for the High School was not realised until 1959.

National Association of High School Pupils

At the end of the 1940's, as so often before, there was talk of a crisis in the Folk High School. The intake of pupils was falling, and there were fears that the situation would worsen further with the migration from country to town. At this stage, there was little communication with the towns, except at a few High Schools such as Krogerup and the Workers High Schools. The majority in the Trade Unions and the Social Democratic Party looked at the High Schools of the time with condescending contempt: they were only for peasants with straw in their clogs. Farmers' children with little schooling!

It was no longer enough to count on an intake of pupils resulting from advertisements in the High School Paper and old pupils' direct recommendation of the High School which they had themselves attended. Far-sighted High School folk understood that there would have to be a collective effort in the towns, through the various High School Associations of pupils. On 28 April 1949, a meeting was held in the Association of High Schools and Agricultural Schools, where the question was discussed of what could be done to establish a basis for contact with the towns. It was agreed that ignorance prevailed in wide circles, or quite inaccurate ideas as to what a term at a High School involved. A five-man committee was set up, which held 3 meetings and submitted a report. Their proposal was that information should be circulated through various channels, and for this a necessary condition was the establishment of a National Association of Pupils.

Now, things began to move. At a meeting in the Association of High Schools and Agricultural Schools on 25/26 October the same year, it was decided to realise the project for a National Association of High School Pupils in Denmark. Its object should be »to work for the benefit of the Danish Folk High School and the High School idea, for example by running the High School Secretariat in co-operation with the Association of Folk High Schools in Denmark«.

The Secretariat was commissioned (1) through radio, films and the press to increase interest in the High School; (2) to seek contact with the evening classes movement; (3) to arrange »High School days« in Copenhagen and other major cities; (4) to negotiate on new arrangements for the High School Paper and (5) if necessary to support the Danish High School in South Slesvig.

All the boards of the pupils associations were asked to decide on joining the national association as soon as possible. The subscription was set at 25 øre per pupil association member. Although this was not an amount which could wreck a budget, with the great High Schools' many pupil association members it amounted to a good deal.

The Constituent General Assembly took place on 12 March 1950. The Board of Directors was constituted with the former Minister of Education, Jørgen Jørgensen, as Chairman. His word carried weight, also outside the High School world. The national association reached a figure of 50,000 members. It joined the children's and youth organisations in the Danish Youth Joint Council, the World Assembly of Youth, and the Association of the Youth Committees of the North. It was also represented in the Brønshøj-Husum Youth House and Danish Cultural Films, and established a contact committee in Copenhagen whose efforts are to constitute a channel of contact and a forum for ideas for the pupils associations. Lastly, the National Association publishes the periodical *High School Pupils*.

On 31 March 1978, the National Association consisted of 28 High School pupils associations.

The High School Secretariat

Among the items on the programme of the National Association, as mentioned above, was the establishment of a secretariat, from which the campaign should be prepared. The High School teacher Erik Halvorsen was appointed secretary, and he proved to be an organiser full of ideas.

Halvorsen had to begin quite modestly by borrowing a desk, with a telephone, in one of the Copenhagen High School Association's premises, of which the association itself had the use in the evenings. Good co-operation was established with the High School Association, which had experience of High School work among circles unfamiliar with the High School. Particularly by holding courses of 8 days' duration. The secretariat later obtained its own office in Vartov's fine old building on the

Town Hall Square in the centre of Copenhagen, and more office staff could be engaged.

Halvorsen published brochures and press announcements of short and long courses at the High Schools, arranged High School evenings with outside lecturers in the factories, and held evening classes at Vartov itself. The secretariat became a permanent institution, of which no one doubted the necessity. This was evident from the many students who came to High Schools, recommended by the secretariat. It was also evident from its many offers of summer schools for participants of all ages.

The secretariat was visited every year by guests from the whole world, who wished to hear about the Danish Folk High Schools and visit them. It received a State allocation from the Ministry of Foreign Affairs, to establish a special *Information Office*. On the recommendation of »the Committee concerning Folk High Schools«, an allowance appears every year in the Budget for the secretariat's work, so that there is a balance between private and public contributions.

In the autumn 1953, unofficial co-operation was started with the Continuation Schools. From May 1964, when the Continuation Schools had a representative in the National Association of High School Pupils, this co-operation became official. It ended on 1 January 1971, when the Continuation Schools established their own secretariat.

The High School Secretariat was also responsible for the High Schools' work for the developing countries, which functioned in the years 1964–66. The Danish developing countries school in Holte, the *Rural Development College,* which was started in 1964 with the support of the developing countries' management, its Principal being Svend Erik Bjerre, was transferred in 1973 to Grundtvig's High School.

At the same time as the National Association of High School Pupils and the High School Secretariat were set up, the High School Fund was established, to give support to pupils wishing to spend a term at High School. Here too, Jørgen Jørgensen was one of the principal moving spirits. The grants are given mainly to young people who have taken part in club work of ideological, religious or other types. The money comes from funds, institutions, etc. The High School Fund is administered through the secretariat with voluntary help. Neither the Board of Directors nor the Selection Committee receive payment for their work, and nor does the Treasurer.

Committee concerning the Folk High School

In 1954, the Ministry of Education set up a *Committee concerning the Folk High School,* with Professor Nyboe Andersen as Chairman. According to its terms of reference, the task of the committee was »to investigate what needs exist in modern society for human and civic instruction, which the Folk High School can give, and what impediments stand in the way of meeting this need to the greatest possible extent. It is expected, especially, that the Committee will describe the Folk High School's attitude towards other forms of adult education, point out such factors in business life and in the labour market as may have an obstructive effect upon access to a stay at a High School, and discuss questions concerning the Folk High School's projects for courses, teaching and other elements which must be assumed to be significant to the school's capacity to complete its task«.

The Committee completed a statistical investigation, the results of which were published in Recommendation No. 178, in 1957. Later the committee issued »Recommendation concerning the Folk High School« (Recommendation No. 261) in 1960.

The intention behind the establishment of the Committee was to make the High Schools' general education available to wider circles than those traditionally interested. There was no question of diminishing intakes of pupils. On the contrary, the latter had been increasing, and could be expected to increase further, when the young people from the last years with a high birthrate from the War, and immediately after, reached High School age. The Committee believed that a better field of contact could be achieved, partly by the spread of knowledge concerning the High Schools and partly by removing some of the obstacles which made attendance at a High School difficult for young people in urban employment.

The Committee found that the adjustment to the urbanization of society should take place on the High Schools' own initiative. It recommended that the work of information on the High Schools, which the High School Secretariat had set in motion in the towns, should be underwritten economically by State aid, and developed further.

In the Committee's view, it was not enough that a High School term was fitted into the training of nurses and kindergarten teachers. It was desirable that it should also be included in apprenticeships, librarian training, and training for the Police and Defence Forces, and recommendations to this effect were made in the proper quarters. These recommendations and the proposal to replace the philosophical test at the university with a term at a High School were received kindly, but non-committally, and were not followed up energetically enough. More contact was needed between the High Schools and the organisations in the towns, and on the labour market. For the young people who were facing a change of employment, it was thought desirable that a High School semester could open up for the possibility of clarifying the individual's plans for the future. In such a case, the teaching staff should be able to help with vocational guidance.

It was emphasized that at a High School, the young people would be able to learn co-operation, while at the same time they developed independence and a sense of responsibility. All of them qualities for which there was use in business or trade, the organisations and political democratic government, and which could be developed better at a High School than through a technical training. Co-operation and democratization must be important targets for the High Schools in the future. The patriarchal situation which had prevailed previously on the farms could no longer be the model for the High Schools. Also a current article by Nyboe Andersen in »The Folk High School in the North. Year book 1960,« called for a freer democratic comradeship between teachers and pupils: »We can hardly send our pupils home from the High Schools with more valuable experience than what they gain during the attempts to get the flock of pupils to work and enjoy themselves in comradeship and free-

118

dom.« A number of the ideas put forward in the recommendation left their mark on later legislation on the High School.

The Scandinavian Seminar

As part of the efforts to give students from abroad the possibility of having a term at a Danish Folk High School, the institution *The Scandinavian Seminar* was started. It was directed at American university students and young people who had finished their education. The administration of the agency work was entrusted to the American-Scandinavian Council for Adult Education, New York. The arrangement involved a 9 months term of study in Denmark, including a semester at a High School. In certain instances this could be recognized as part of a university education, so that the total period of study would not be prolonged.

The Scandinavian Seminar, which is a private foundation, was originally started as an experiment. After the arrangement had worked satisfactorily in Denmark for 4 years, the programme was extended in 1963 to the whole of Scandinavia, so that pupils had freedom of choice between one of the 3 Scandinavian countries or Finland.

No knowledge of any of the Nordic languages is required before an application is sent in. Seminars consist of 5 parts: (1) short concentrated language courses, lectures and discussions, (2) family visits of 4–9 weeks, (3) a High School course of at least 5 months, (4) the writing of a paper on an assignment in the pupil's particular field set by and sent in to their university, (5) an account of what has been gained during the term of study.

The assignment for the university can be chosen from within all areas of cultural life. For students in Denmark, the following are examples: Runic inscriptions – the history of the Home Mission and its social effects – Danish pottery, past and present – Denmark and the Common Market – the Folk High School concept, as it has been realised – the history of Greenland from 1721 – reflections on Kierkegaard themes – social welfare for the aged, etc.

Experience has shown that most pupils achieve much greater proficiency in reading, speaking and writing in a Scandinavian language than they would be able to gain at a 2 or 3-year language course in their own country. From the moment they set foot on foreign soil, the new language begins to live for them, and when they return home, their ability to express themselves is often surprisingly good.

One important aim of the seminar is to activate the pupil and to strengthen his/her self-confidence and self-discipline. An additional aim is that the pupils, by entering into a way of life so vastly different from their own, can gain new, and deeper, insight into their own culture and a better understanding of the world as a whole.

Since 1950/51, 75–100 American pupils have come to High Schools in the Scandinavian countries and Finland every year, through the Scandinavian Seminar.

The North

In all this, however, Nordic co-operation was not forgotten. The traditional summer meetings of Nordic High School folk were resumed after the War and held in Denmark, Norway, Finland and Sweden in turn. *The Nordic Folk High School Council* was founded with the task of preparing and organising these meetings, which have taken place every third year since 1945. The Council has gradually taken over all questions relating to this co-operation. Most years since 1960 it has published »The Folk High School in the North«, which includes a resumé in English for the information of folk enlightenment circles outside Scandinavia.

In 1947, the *Nordiska Folkhögskolan* (Nordic Folk High School) was opened in Kungälv, near Göteborg, and in 1960 the *Nordens Folkhögskola Biskops-Arnö* (Bishop Arnö Folk High School of the North) near Uppsala, both with capacity for 70 pupils.

The Nordic Folk High School in Kungälv was established in an old mansion at the foot of the Fontinbjerg. The start of the school was made possible by support from Kungälv town and various private sources. From the beginning, importance was attached in teaching to social orientation, with the North as the point of gravity, including literary and aesthetic subjects relating to this, in Nordic languages. In addition to the Swedish teachers, one teacher from each of the other Nordic countries was attached to the High School.

The Bishop Arnö Folk High School of the North, lying amid beautiful scenery near Mälaren, is owned by the *Norden Association*. Here too, emphasis is laid on Nordic languages and Nordic literature. Instruction in the orientation subjects takes the form, to some extent, of projects covering several subjects.

In 1968, the Nordic Folk High School in Kungälv moved into a new building up on the Fontinbjerg itself, with a view over the Bohus fortress by the Göta river, where the frontiers of Denmark, Norway and Sweden once met. Here *Nordens folkliga Akademi* (the Folk Academy of the North) was also housed.

The idea of a joint Nordic academy was originally Grundtvig's, but it was not until 100 years later, in 1938, that his idea was taken up to actual discussion at ministerial level. The War put a stop to these discussions, but after the establishment of the *Nordic Council* in 1953, a committee of experts was set up, which recommended a folk academy, although not quite as Grundtvig had intended. The academy was to be started as a joint institution for the Nordic folk and states, attached to the Folk High Schools already in existence. In 1964, the Nordic Governments appointed a Board of Directors, which formulated the aims of the academy:

»The Folk Academy of the North shall be a centre for the study of questions which are relevant to the development and renewal of the work of Nordic folk enlightenment. The activity of the Academy shall be oriented especially to teachers and leaders of Folk High Schools, and free and voluntary folk education and youth work. In its work the Academy shall strive to develop understanding both of the multifarious joint elements in the culture and society of the North and of the co-operation of the North with the rest of the world.«

The official opening took place on 7 June 1968, with speeches by the then Swedish Minister of Education, Oluf Palme, the former Danish Minister of Education, Jørgen Jørgensen, and the French Professor Erica Simon.

The small closed society on the Fontinbjerg is occupied, apart from the High School pupils, by participants in the various short courses of the Academy – maximum 40 – as well as teachers and other permanent staff. The Academy has lecturers from the Nordic countries, among them, at the time of writing, a former Principal, the Swede Björn Höjer. Visiting teachers also come from the whole of Scandinavia. Courses are held throughout the year, except in the summer holidays.

The Folk Academy of the North has become a meeting-place for discussions and exchange of ideas on the basis of folk enlightenment – for the people and about the people. It has been a source of inspiration, therefore, even if it does not conform so much to Grundtvig's »Göteborg idea« as to his other ideas on folk enlightenment.

Youth High Schools

In 1963, an energetic educationalist, Jens Kr. la Cour Madsen, began an experiment at his Continuation School at Ribe with a form of High School teaching, especially adapted for 16 to 19-year-old pupils. Aid to the pupils was made contingent upon how far a pupil was of Continuation School or High School age. He noticed that there was far greater difference in maturity between the 17-year-olds and the majority of the Continuation School clientele of 15 to 16-year-olds than had been realised previously. He therefore proposed the establishment of a new High School form, intended for those who felt too grown-up to go to Continuation School, and yet were too young to be able to obtain aid for a High School term. This was a neglected age group, and the few who went to High School constituted an immature appendage. A sample excerpt from the figures for 1964/65 shows the following age divisions:

Continuation School pupils	16 years of age and under ...	45%
Continuation School pupils	17 years	5%
High School pupils	17 years	4%
High School pupils	18 years of age and over	46%
In all		*100%*

The Ministry of Education decided that la Cour Madsen's application for approval for a special Youth High School for the neglected age group, was well founded, as it was at the free schools that the demands of modern society for the ability to co-operate were taken into consideration. In 1965, his school was approved as a combined High School and Continuation School, for pupils between 17 and 19 years of age, on condition that it was designated as a Youth High School. In the years that followed, other Youth High Schools were started, some of which have since been closed. On 1 January 1977, in addition to the *Youth High School at Ribe*, a Youth High School was approved in *Egå* near Århus, and another at *Andebølle* on Funen. The Youth High Schools have been attended by 300–400 pupils a year. Most of these have finished the 10th form or the 3rd secondary school form. Nearly all come direct from school, with no interval in a job or in the ordinary life of society. The length of the courses varies from 16 to 32 weeks, and are regarded by the pupils as part of a year of waiting before they start on their advanced education. Young people who are not yet 17, but have finished the 10th form, are included in the number of »year's pupils«.

Since the curriculum of the Youth High Schools to some extent resembles that of the High Schools, their administration follows approximately the rules for Folk High Schools. This means that the pupils who belong to the age group eligible for Continuation School grants can follow the same rules for grants as do the Folk High School pupils. There is no access – as there is at Continuation Schools – to examinations.

VIII.

PROFILE OF THE 1970's

Society and the High School

There was a marked tendency in Denmark in the 1970's to give greater weight to what was »European« than to what was national particularly after NORDEK (Nordic Economic Cooperation) was abandoned, and when Denmark joined the Common Market in 1972, which lessened interest in Nordic orientation still further. The sense of being European, before being conscious of one's Nordic identity made itself felt more and more in politically influential circles. This was a tendency which Grundtvig, in his time, had fought against with all his strength. This internationalism, which manifested itself within the High School world, for example in the 16th edition of the High School Song Book of 1974, in which old tried patriotic songs had to give place to songs and verses in foreign languages, was easy to explain. It was natural that a reaction must come against the overemphasis of a nationalism which could bring such extreme consequences as Europe had suffered in this century.

At the same time, however, polarization took place within Danish society, splitting it into political wings without sufficient feeling for the interdependence of the population, and its common responsibility. The right wing was represented by the »Party of the Future«, which on the basis of a radical liberal viewpoint demanded that nothing must check private initiative. The left wing (the Communist Party and especially the intellectual »elite« among the left wing socialists) rejected middle-class society, together with the »one-dimensional person«. These two extremes had one thing in common: suspicion of the people and contempt for the old parliamentary parties. Social solidarity (or to use a Grundtvig expression, »likeness to the people«) had to yield to group solidarity. This was reflected in the High Schools' differentiation. (The latest branch on the tree was a Women's High School with a clearly feminist character).

Earlier, practically all High Schools were rooted in the philosophy of liberalism. An exception to this was provided by the LO (Trade Unions) High Schools, where liberalism had received a layer of social democratic varnish, but without civic values being attacked. Now came a change. The High School Act of 1970 made it easier to start new untraditional High Schools, and some of them built on the new Marxist ideology of the Student Revolution. According to this, a High School should be socially critical, i.e. elucidate social problems on the basis of a radically critical attitude to the present social system and possibly point to other possibilities. In answer to this, the supporters of the time-honoured High School viewpoint maintained that what the social critics aimed at was social criticism alone, in the sense that they rejected what they wished to criticise, before even starting to analyse it. In reply to this, the social critics pointed to the role which the High Schools had played in the period of the provisional laws, when so many High School men actively supported the Left Wing Opposition's criticism of the reactionary political system. In those days, the Folk High School had had influence on the life of the people. Supporters of the traditional High School maintained, however, in proper Grundtvigian spirit, that its influence had been indirect, and that what the radical social critics were aiming at was direct influence. Yes, and not only that. For them it was essential that the pupils become engaged in a very definite attitude, with political intent.

The Travelling High School

Among the High Schools aiming at an alternative social system was the Travelling High School, one of the »Tvind« schools.

Their authority is the paragraph on research in the High School Act of 1970, according to which theoretical teaching can be combined with practical work, including production, if required, and which reads in part:

»Where teaching has aimed chiefly at participants storing up what they have learned, the teaching may now aim at what is learned being put into practice. Where teaching has taken place mainly in the schoolroom, it may now also take place outside it. At the grocer's, in the office, in the factory. Neither in its content nor by its methods may teaching hide the fact that people do not stand alone, but together, as regards existence. It is therefore one of the principal purposes of teaching to contribute in practice to the ability of participants to co-operate in a joint aim.«

These educational principles, aimed at the target of project-oriented group work, were not only practised at Tvind, Kolding High School, the Red High School, the High School of the Day, the Little High School and other High Schools aiming at an alternative society, but also at many pluralistic schools. The characteristic feature of the Travelling High School was an autocratic structure, camouflaged by the tone of comradeship between teachers and pupils, which enabled the leaders to keep a firm grip on decision-making within a collective system. This necessitated a strict moral code, based on the fact that the commune worked towards a definite aim, which all were interested in attaining and must therefore be willing to accept some group pressure. Should disagreement arise between an individual and the commune, the rights of the commune would in all cases take priority.

At the Travelling High School, participants in the commune have to prepare and carry out journeys, preferably to a Third World country. At the time of writing, the school functions as follows: Before applications for a course are accepted, some of the school's teachers – »veterans« – hold preliminary meetings with those possibly interested in joining. These can then decide whether they are prepared to adjust themselves to the conditions of the commune and to a rigorous ban on couples living together and on alcohol.

During a course, important decisions in the commune are taken at joint meetings (decisions on expulsion for bad behaviour, assignment of work such as cooking and cleaning, maintenance and building work, accounts, budgetting, etc.). Since unanimity is required, and not simply an ordinary majority, these meetings can be lengthy, before an obstinate minority, with a different opinion from that of the majority, give in.

A course lasts 9 months, the first two of which are occupied with preparations for the journey. A group of 8–10 participants, including two »veterans« get hold of an old discarded bus or motor coach, which they overhaul themselves and fit up with sleeping bunks. The bus journey lasts 4 months and involves very close contact between the members of the bus group. None of them are allowed to be alone for very long. The forced collectivism brings many demanding social processes into action. Not everyone can cope with a course with the Travelling High School. The last three months are used for working with the material collected, and the experiences gained, supplemented with comparisons with conditions in Denmark.

To judge from the books used, on history and social orientation, criticism of the prevalent division of power and property in the world is a main purpose of the work of the Travelling High School. It is for this reason, particularly, that the bus journeys to countries of the Third World are educational and important. At the same time, the Travelling High School has succeeded, by its puritanical and restrictive, but clearly comprehensible rules, in solving educational problems where the traditional school system has had to admit defeat.

The High School was started in 1970, in very modest conditions, in hired rooms at the Rantzausminde Continuation School near Svendborg. Among the founders were Mogens Amdi Petersen and the present principal Poul Jørgensen. After a »touchdown« on Fanø Island, the school moved in 1972 to Tvind near Ulfborg, into houses which the teachers and pupils built themselves. A Teachers College and a Continuation School were established in connexion with the High School, and run on the same educational lines, with a mixture of theory and practice. Later, more Tvind schools were started in various places in Denmark. On 1 January 1980, Tvind consisted of 3

High Schools, a Teachers College, 7 Continuation Schools, a Free School, a Seamen's School and Svendborg Steam Mill, also fitted up as a school, with a total of about 200 teachers. In addition, the group ran a business with occupation for young unemployed, a publishing house, some farms, fruit farms, a shipping company, etc. As a concrete argument in the debate on alternative energy, they have built the world's largest windmill. This gave the movement self-confidence. The work of building the mill was carried out by four of the teachers from the school, and voluntary helpers from outside the school. This meant considerable savings. The necessary expertise was provided by Denmark's Technical University. The mill was inaugurated in the spring 1978.

At the New Year 1979, the concern owned buildings and other property amounting to over 50 million kroner. This expansion was largely financed by the Tvind Teachers Savings Association, to which the teachers pay in their entire salaries, minus taxes and an amount for necessary private expenses. Some of the teachers have even put their capital into the savings association. Teachers cannot withdraw their savings if they leave the school. The savings association gives loans, free of interest, to the mother company of the Tvind concern, a private foundation called *Common Property*, which is run by 5–7 veterans. Common Property owns the buildings and the shipping firm via co-operative societies.

At the Tvind schools, the *Teaching Group* is the official supreme authority. Its meetings are held in private. Only the teachers are admitted, and no minutes are allowed. Some of the meetings are only for the senior teachers. They alone know what has taken place, and what decisions have been taken at all the meetings. But all proposals for the agenda must first be approved by the *Co-ordinating Group*, which consists of the top men in the Tvind hierarchy, who also decide who is to take the Chair at the meetings of the Teaching Group.

Tvind schools are among the institutions which have received EEC grants to combat unemployment among young people.

The Travelling High School in Tvind, which is only one piece in the mosaic of the concern, as mentioned already, has been the

Folk High School which in the financial year 1976/77 had the largest intake of pupils. The competition from the Travelling High School is evident in the diminishing intake of pupils at several of the older High Schools.

Co-operation Difficulties

With the general rise in the standard of living, High School pupils have been able to allow themselves a personal consumption which would have astonished the High School pupils of earlier times. But sometimes, dissatisfaction and a feeling of being badly treated followed in the wake of the improved material conditions, and this manifested itself in that they refused to accept things as they were, and sometimes led to an acute contrast between considerations of the common good and the size of the individual's demands.

In the years around 1970, serious crises arose at Ryslinge, Askov, Brejdablik and several other High Schools. But it was only the co-operation difficulties at the three above schools which gave rise to detailed press reports. At Ryslinge High School, activists, backed up by a minority of the teachers, made a wild attack on the person of the Principal and the attitude of the school. The then Director for Youth Instruction from the Ministry of Education had to break off his summer holidays to mediate between the conflicting parties. In vain. With regard to the new High School Act which was imminent at the time, he told the Press that a High School must make an visible effort to encourage pupils to take on their share of responsibility for the running of the school. It was not until the end of the school term that the affair quietened down, and an arrangement which was satisfactory to the Principal was reached.

At Ryslinge, the Principal had the support of the Board of Directors. This was also the case at some other High Schools where co-operation difficulties led to the dismissal of some of the teachers. But at Askov High School, Brejdablik High School (since closed) and West Jutland's High School it was the Principal who was dismissed. Since the disturbances, particularly at

Askov and Brejdablik, affected the High Schools generally thereafter – although in different fields – a short account of it will be given:

In October 1970, the Principal of Askov High School had to resign after pressure from the Board of Directors. One of the main reasons for this was serious disagreement in the Teachers Council, on how the school should function. The Principal supported a minority group of teachers who opposed the traditional view of the treatment of the school curriculum. The disagreement finally crystallized in a general debate on the principle of whether a High School should seek to influence pupils directly or indirectly: whether teachers should engage the pupils in quite definite viewpoints or run the school so as to inspire the pupils to make up their own minds on their standpoints. This also became a controversial question in the rest of the High School world. In the spring 1971, the Board of Directors succeeded in filling the position of Principal with a former Askov teacher. The eight teachers in the minority group, who had protested against the dismissal of the Principal, agreed to resign, with economic compensation. In 1972, five of them started the radical social critical High School in Kolding. This, like the Tvind schools, was built by teachers and pupils.

In December 1970, both the Principal and the teachers at Brejdablik were dismissed. The Board of Directors found that the Principal had to live up to his duty as set out in his terms of reference, to run the school as a High School with advanced instruction. Protests from the pupils and others gave rise to a question in Parliament to the Ministry of Education, who replied in part:

»The Board of Directors have the responsibility for the ideology on which the school, according to its statutes, has based its work, really being complied with, and this responsibility can in certain cases necessitate the dismissal of one or more teachers, including the school Principal. The Board of Directors are responsible for the economy of the school and are personally liable for errors of judgement, in accordance with the general rules of compensation under Danish law. For this reason also, the Board of Directors shall have the possibility of dismissing the Principal.

»The free schools offer a number of forms of instruction. It is up to the individual pupil to choose between schools. By his choice, however, the pupil must have made up his mind as to the lines on which the school shall be run, and have the right to expect that these lines are followed . . .«

In principle, the Board of Directors, as representatives of the tax payers, who pay 85% of the running costs of the High Schools, have a free hand to lay down the objectives of the individual school. To carry out these objectives, it chooses a Principal, who in his turn chooses his teachers, all of them free within the framework of the objectives. The free hand of the Board of Directors consists, for example, in being able to choose a new Principal, if it does not consider the previous Principal pursues the school's objectives.

The Psychological Deviates

Internal conflict was not the only symptom of the crisis in the High School world which the Youth Revolution in 1968 had provoked. The difficulties were accentuated by deviating pupils, with adjustment and co-operation problems, a number of them drink or narcotic addicts. Among them there were some who had come to High School at their own or their parents' wishes, but the great majority had been sent there by Social Service authorities. Many High School people were afraid that, if the debate on job satisfaction, which spread in the wake of the Youth Revolution, also included a therapeutic environment at the expense of education, they would run into incalculable problems. But according to the Social Service authorities sending them, the psychologically handicapped young people needed periods at High School more than did others. They would be able to develop their personalities, and so strengthen their sense of belonging to humanity and to society.

In September 1970, a conference was held for the exchange of orientation and experience, between teachers and principals on the one side, and on the other, representatives for the child and juvenile welfare authorities, rehabilitation, prison, vocational guidance administrations, school psychologists, etc. The discussions concluded in an application to the Ministry of Education, which appointed a contact committee the same year, to examine the problems of the pupils in question. According to its terms of reference, the committee had 3 tasks: (1) to be a forum for contact between the schools and the personnel of the authorities referred to; (2) to publish printed matter of an informative nature; and (3) to arrange courses and conferences as required.

The Committee held a number of meetings, particularly in the first years, when the High Schools' problems with narcotic addicts culminated. In 1972, a publication was issued entitled »Report of Referring Authorities, etc.«. Here the Child and Juvenile Welfare Service, the Danish Public Assistance Service, the Prison Service, Rehabilitation, the Public Vocational Guidance Service and the School Psychological Counsel Service gave information on their activities, intended for school staffs. On 1 April 1976, when the new Public Assistance Act came into force, most of these tasks were transferred to the local authorities, so that the report became obsolete. The composition of the Committee had to be altered, and a new publication was issued. In 1977 »Statement for Guidance in Co-operation between the Social and Health Services and the Folk High Schools, Domestic Science Schools, and Continuation Schools« came out, for the information of all the parties concerned.

The question of admittance of narcotic addicts to the High Schools was discussed in the High School Paper. All the High School folk were agreed on taking steps to combat the abuse of alcohol, and that hash and other euphoriants should not be tolerated in any circumstances. However, they did not oppose the admittance of problem pupils in principle, when these were referred to the High Schools by the authorities, but the numbers must be limited to between 5% and 10%, if the boarding school environment was not to suffer. There was general agreement that even if it was a question of free schools, which received considerable State grants, the decision was their own as to which pupils they were willing to accept, and they also prepared their own teaching. The refusal of a pupil could be a lesser evil than expulsion, which would simply be felt as a new defeat by the person involved. Lastly it should not be forgotten that a High School was an educational centre, not a nursing home.

Although, traditionally, there was also room for deviates and social losers, there were some High Schools at the beginning of the 1970's which found it necessary to send detailed application forms to those wishing to become their pupils. Sometimes the applicants were sent for to have talks with the Principal and staff, before their acceptance was decided upon. A factor in this decision was that a High School was also a private firm which needed pupils to make its existence economically possible, but that it would be unfortunate if it allowed itself to be used as an institution for the dregs of society, for economic reasons. If social educational problems were to dominate the daily life of the High Schools, their identity would gradually be erased.

Conflict between the Old and the New

As mentioned above, there were also High Schools with no radical socially critical aim, which to a greater or lesser extent abandoned the educational system of teacher-centred classes. In the High School world, too, the demand for grass roots democracy was the solution of the 1970's. The new ideas in education were reflected in zealous young High School teachers' use of language, where expressions and turns of phrase were borrowed from the exaggerations of psychology. The word »comradeship« had been worn thin during the 1960's. Now one said that people »should matter to each other« to »get it up on its feet«. The air buzzed with expressions such as »anti-authoritarian pedagogics«, »break down all the barriers between teachers and pupils«, »activization through group-dynamic work«. Above all, it was a question of »don't let them pull the wool over your eyes«.

On a line with other school forms, phased, largely thematic, and especially inter-disciplinary forms of work were introduced. The inter-disciplinary themes gave a broader view and more coherence, and stimulated the pupils to joint activity. But they could not stand alone. They weakened the educational value of a thorough, basic impartation of knowledge, and had to be supplemented with teaching in study groups. In addition, group work often entailed hours of fruitless discussion before a start could be made, and it made great demands upon the patience, interest, and abilities of many pupils. The decisive point, however, was that inspiration should go out from the pupil more than from the teacher, who should simply have a consultative function. There were only a few of the teachers of the time who were able to meet the demands of group work, with the inspirational, narrative, and at the same time factually informative lecture form, ex catedra.

There were High Schools where teachers and pupils joined forces in all the work which the boarding school form necessitated. Not only cleaning, cooking and other kitchen work, but also brick-laying, carpentry and maintenance work. Like the Travelling High School. Unlike it, however, these High Schools had many single rooms and offered the individual pupil considerable freedom, with very liberal rules, decided upon by the pupils themselves, without much interference from above.

It was not only educational aims which lay behind these reforms, however. There were also reasons of economy. The pupils received a share of responsibility for the running of the school, also from the point of view of economy. This was possible, for one thing because many of the pupils who went to High School in the 1970's had become used to taking active part in the processes of decision, from their earlier school days. They were prepared in advance, to commit themselves and have a voice in common problems.

The teachers could go a long way in their efforts to include the pupils in the choice of material and subjects. Sometimes a certain sum would be set aside for study tours and leisure activities, after which it was left to the pupils to administer the money themselves. They had the right to a vote on a question up to the point where they collided with the regulations in the instruments of a school foundation, or the whole teaching programme, or where the right of voting on a question was limited by the Principal's (or staff's) economic responsibilities. Important decisions were taken at joint meetings, in which pupils, teachers and the rest of the school personnel took part. There were pupils meetings, teachers meetings, group meetings, corridor meetings, committee meetings, co-ordinating meetings, etc. etc. Much of this meeting activity was time-consuming to the point of parody. Inspiration and initiative should come largely from the pupils. The teacher's function was of a more consultative nature. But if too high a priority was given to pupils' self-government, a school could become slack. The image of the individual school's special character and line, established by its reputation, could be blurred. Malicious tongues even accused some individual High Schools of being market places for the passing fancies of dominating groups of pupils.

Far from all the High Schools went so far in their efforts towards democracy. Curricula, communal existence and aims varied from one school to another. Most of the High Schools belonged to the comfortable average, with pluralistic observance, and there were even High Schools where the effort was to preserve the traditional sovereignty of the Principal; but on the opposing wing there were also High Schools which were run collectively, although in such instances, one teacher had to represent the school *vis-à-vis* the Ministry. But in that case he only had a purely juridical responsibility. At Kolding High School, the teachers took it in turns to be Principal, for one year at a time. Also elsewhere, it became more and more common for the Principal to be changed after a few years. The Principal's name and personality did not represent the school in people's minds to the extent that they had done previously. The cult of personality was finished. No High School dynasties arose, such as the Schrøder and Appel families at Askov, and the Triers at Vallekilde. They belonged to a past age. The High Schools had become institutions.

As a result of the new High Schools' breadth, and the polarization of society, the High Schools became more and more differentiated. Nevertheless, they shared a common feature which divided them from other school forms. Factual and human knowledge could certainly be had just as well or better at other schools, many of which had better teachers than the High Schools. But at a High School, the pupils and staff lived in close contact with each other for shorter or longer periods. A special feature of the High School was also the way in which problems

135

were presented, on the background of the teachers' and pupils' experience and home conditions. A particularly valuable side was conversation, which continued after the classes, during meals, and in the pupils' rooms. The boarding school form was therefore an indispensable factor in the educational activity as a whole. There was a need for the home-like character which Kold stressed, and Grundtvig's »living interchange«. However, the five-day week and motorization were a threat to the boarding school environment.

There were collisions between the old and the new. The High Schools' conditions in the 1970's were different from those in 1945. The structural changes took place in such rapid succession that the High Schools found it difficult to keep up with them, if Schrøder's words, that the High Schools' work was at the point where the teachers' abilities and the pupils' needs met, should maintain their validity. In the many small farming and artisan businesses and shops, the home and the place of work had been part of each other, but now the family only functioned during leisure hours, and no longer as a production unit. Young people took less part in the daily production, but had many years of schooling before they went to High School. After the High School term, few of the pupils returned to their previous jobs, but went on to advanced education. The situation where a student preferred the manual High School subjects recurred again and again. It showed that he/she also needed to see the results of practical work, and was not powerless, but could complete concrete tasks, which he had chosen himself, and thus help to influence his surroundings. For some this was a good antidote to school fatigue, for others a protest against the specialized society's monotonous work, where one had no share in forming the final product. Many young High School folk were influenced by the Marxist view of work, according to which a person expresses himself, and so to speak creates himself, makes himself a person through his work, through the material production of the necessities of life. Marx claimed that by being able to visualize the result of a piece of work beforehand, planning and gathering experience, man lifts himself above the beasts, who only have an instinctive relationship to work. And as a High School man expressed it: »In the High School context, one can quite well cultivate the interplay between the *living word* and the *living* (i.e. made living, meaningful) *work*.[1]

Askov High School's Working Programme

Among the High Schools which held fast to the traditional work forms, and did not embark on educational experiments, letting the pupils do the cooking, brick-laying and painting, was Askov. This was evident from the following weekly time table:

A. *Teaching*
The pupils themselves decide their time table, which – when it has been approved by the school – is in force until another arrangement is agreed. Changes in the time table can only take place by agreement with the teacher in question, and with the Principal's approval. However, each pupil must choose a suitable working programme of about 20 hours a week, and follow it regularly and actively.

If a pupil fails to attend classes without sufficient reason, the teacher can state that the pupil's participation in the group has come to an end. If the pupil's attendance falls below the minimum programme, the conditions for his remaining at the school will normally have ended.

Illness must be reported to the school nurse. If a pupil is otherwise prevented from attending a single class, the pupil must inform the teacher. If absence from the school involves non-attendance at classes, the permission of the Principal must be obtained.

B. *General subjects* (the weekly hours are given in brackets)
Library course (1 hour) – Games (2 hours) – Philosophy (2 hours) – Foreign languages: English, French or German (3 hours) – Gymnastics (3 hours) – Orchestra (2 hours) – Choral singing (2 hours) – Mathematics II (2 hours) – Mathematics III (2 hours) – Musical appreciation (1 hour) – Arithmetic (2 hours) – Grammar (2 hours) – Analysis of material (3 hours).

C. *Special Groups*
Include a number of groups which meet on Wednesday afternoons. The following are available: Plant dyes – Pottery – Drama practice – Photography – Electrotechnology.

---

1. Vilhelm Nielsen: »The Folk High School between Grundtvig and Marx«. (Grundtvig och folkupplysningen. Nordens folkliga Akademi, 1978. S. 71–82).

D. *Danish Literature*

A number of groups are available, each of which work 3 times a week. There are various types of group. Further information on arrival.

E. *Social Problems*

A number of groups are available, each of which work 3 times a week. On arrival at the school there will be an opportunity to choose between various subjects.

F. *Lectures. Orientation*

In addition to the instruction given in small classes, and of which a number aim at meeting the pupils' special interests, some hours per week of the school time table are reserved for lectures. Added to these there are a number of hours with guest lecturers from outside the permanent school staff. The purpose of the lectures is to present subjects of a topical and general character in an overall perspective or from a particular viewpoint. As an alternative teaching form they give everyone at the school the possibility of choosing within a common field of material. In addition there are orientation classes and debates, led by members of the staff or guest lecturers, on various subjects, including the most topical.

G. *Study Groups*

The study groups include more specialized subjects. Pupils make their choice during the first few days. The study groups fall into 3 categories, one of which is planned to run throughout the winter. Within this category's *long group* every pupil will be able to choose to take part in one subject. The second category consists of 3-months study groups, which will later be replaced with new offers. In this category of *half-length study groups* it will be possible to choose a subject for each 3-month period. The third category includes both a short and a long study group. The short group works for a 2-month period in November and December, and is replaced after the New Year by a 4-month group. In this category, also, a subject can be chosen for each period.

Study Group I A (from November 1977 to 31 January 1978)

Danish political history 1945–47 – Weaving – Problems of the developing countries, a new economic world order? – Pottery – Folk tales – Musical appreciation – Fundamental religious concepts – Denmark, Scandinavia and Europe – Film analysis, film evaluation – The energy crisis from the ecological viewpoint – European drama.

Study Group II (from November 1977 to 21 April 1978)

The past around us – Thought and philosophy of life in ancient China, India and Europe – Danish economic policy – Psychology of personality – History of ideas – Ideology and cultural policy – Philosophy of life in the novel – The mass media and the formation of opinion – Jazz and Beat music – Mathematics.

Hour	Monday	Tuesday	Wednesday	Thursday	Friday	Saturday
7.45	BREAKFAST					
8.10	SONG					
8.30 9.45	Study group I	Study group II	Study group I	Study group II	Study group I	Study group II
10.00 10.45	Musical appreciation	Lecture	Lecture	Lecture	Study group I	Gymnastics
11.10 12.30	Danish literature I Social Science II	Social Science I Danish literature II Danish for foreigners	Danish Literature I Social Science II	Social Science I Danish literature II Danish for foreigners	–	Orientation foreign politics
12.30	LUNCH					
13.00					House meeting	
14.00 14.45	Danish grammar Material analysis Maths. II	Library course Singing Maths. II	S P E C I	Danish literature I Social Science II	Social Science I Danish literature II	
15.00 15.45	Foreign languages	Orchestra	A L G R	Danish grammar Singing Material analysis	Co-operation Ctee. meeting	
16.00 16.45	Study group III	Philosophy Orchestra Arithmetic	O U P S	Material analysis Arithmetic Philosophy	Study group III	
17.00 17.45	Study group III	Foreign languages Philosophy Gymnastics	–	Gymnastics Foreign languages Philosophy	Study group III	
18.00	SUPPER					
Evening	Folk dancing	19.30–21 Games				»Klem« (pupils' entertainment)

Study Group IIIA (from November 1977 to 31 December 1977)
Blicher and Poul Martin Møller studied on the cultural historical background –
Spinning on a spindle – The creation and development of the new China –
Book-keeping – Drawing – Life ideals and architecture – Revolutionary move-
ments past and present – The conflict between art and life as a theme in poetry.

Study Group I B (from February to 21 April 1978)
Danish foreign policy during the last 100 years – Weaving – Growth or zero-
growth? – Pottery – The child in society – Musical information – What is
Christianity? – From here where we stand – Astronomy – Major dramatic
works.

Study Group III B (from January to 21 April 1978)
Housing – Drawing – Book-keeping – Psychology – The visual arts – Existen-
tialism, literature and policy.

Trade Unions High Schools

Among the High Schools of the 1970's, which did not have an
alternative society on their programme, were the Trade Unions
schools: the High Schools mentioned earlier, in Esbjerg,
re-opened in 1955, Roskilde, re-opened in 1976, and also the LO
(Danish Federation of Trade Unions) School, started in Helsingør in 1969. They went in for the further development of the
social system which the Social Democrat Trade Unions movement stood for. The school therefore experimented with
pupil-centred activity pedagogics and away from the
teacher-centred lecture form towards group work, project-oriented teaching and independent activity. But pupils and
participants in courses were not allowed to take part in building
or painting projects or cultivate bio-dynamic vegetables as part
of the teaching programme.

On the background of the basic view that the capitalist aristocracy had long since given place to an aristocracy of knowledge, it was concrete knowledge of modern society, and not
some form of »upbringing« or indoctrination, which must be the
main purpose of the High School work.

In the 1970's the Trade Unions High Schools concentrated
particularly training shop stewards and political representatives. In the renewal which this necessitated, and the change in
structuralization of the working programme, the Trade Unions

were brought into the foreground. As it was not possible for shop stewards of a certain age to give up time to follow courses of fairly long duration, a broad programme of short courses was introduced, in addition to the compulsory 20-week courses for young people. The short courses were organised to allow the shop stewards to carry through the same educational programme in the same number of weeks but spread over 3–4 years. The typical participant in such courses was 40 years of age, with only 7 years' schooling. He therefore had a considerable lag to catch up, in comparison with the young people with their longer schooling.

Great importance was attached to the course participants learning to formulate their thoughts verbally, and acquire skills in meeting and negotiating techniques, labour legislation, the problems of the labour market, agreements and international co-operation. Actual teaching in artistic or creative subjects took a back seat, but the Workers' Song Book and cultural arrangements received a central position.

The point of departure was that the right of voting, which had won through, more than 100 years ago in the country, in parish councils, and in the co-operative movement, was now also beginning to come to the fore in co-operative committees, company boards of directors and other forms of co-ownership and co-responsibility in the larger firms. It was important that the shop stewards should be equipped to take up these challenges.

From about 1970, the largest Trade Unions established their own schools, with the same type of teaching as the Social Democrat Workers High Schools, but without the long 20-week courses and therefore without State grants under the High School Act.

Pensioners High Schools

The Pensioners High Schools were an answer to the age divisions in the population and the changes of structure in society. In 1975, between one-fifth and one-sixth of the population of Denmark were pensioners. Parents no longer lived with their children and grandchildren, as they had done in the old peasant

141

society. This was inconvenient in the modern urbanized society, because people's homes were not suited to it, if for no other reason. Society took over the social obligations for older people which before had been shouldered by their children. And with the rapid technical developments, generations often grew away from each other to a considerable degree. The average expectation of life had risen, and the older generation remained healthy longer than in earlier times. But with the atomization of society, they often suffered from loneliness. Many had a natural need for the comradeship which could be found at a High School, and in the discussions of later years on lifelong educational activity, the idea was raised of starting Pensioners High Schools.

The Pensioners High Schools were the last brick in the structure which grew from the short summer courses on High School lines of which Holger Begtrup laid the foundation at Frederiksborg High School in 1911. He wished to strengthen the connexion between the Folk High School and their friends in the towns. Later, other High Schools started 8 to 14-day courses on this model. But the actual pensioners courses were held for the first time in 1928 at Esbjerg Workers High School for a week in August. No further interest was shown in the project for the next 30 years. It was not until 1960 that Brandbjerg High School began holding summer courses for pensioners. Other High Schools soon followed suit.

In 1967 the organisation the *Pensioners Co-operative* was started, and under the terms of the Education Act of 4 June 1970 regarding Folk High Schools, Agricultural Schools, Domestic Science Schools and Continuation Schools, special Pensioners High Schools could also obtain recognition as Folk High Schools. According to this law, the Minister of Education can give dispensation from the requirement that to be entitled to State aid, a High School must have carried out a course of at least 20 weeks' duration or 2 courses of at least 12 weeks' duration. The provision for dispensation in the law was intended for High Schools which aimed solely at holding short courses for senior citizens. The Pensioners High Schools, where the idea was to concentrate the teaching in 14-day courses, were thus placed on the same footing as other Folk High Schools.

In 1971, the *Jutland Pensioners High School* at Nørre Nissum was approved. This was started by 1) a group of local folk, most of them teachers at the Teachers Training College, and 2) joint care organisations. The nucleus in the school building was a private college, which could be taken into use after minor alterations and additions. The same year, *Kolt High School for Senior Citizens* was recognized, as a development of a local Free and Continuation School tradition, as was the *Marielyst Pensioners High School* (Falster), which had been bought for holding courses, in 1969, by the Pensioners' Co-operative. Lastly, the resort hotel, *Rude Strand*, south of Århus, bought as a course centre by the organisation *The Co-operative Pensioners' Unions in Denmark*, was approved in 1973 as a Pensioners High School.

The Unemployed at High School

After a number of years with high employment, from 1974, unemployment again began to rise in Denmark. As in the 1930's, support was also given this time for High School terms for the unemployed. On 15 October 1974, a circular was sent out by the Labour Department on the payment of unemployment benefits during a term at High School. The right to benefits was conditional on (a) that the recipient was actively seeking employment and willing to break off the High School term if it was offered him; (b) that the Labour Exchange was informed that he was at High School and in the opinion of the Labour Exchange there was no immediate likelihood that employment would be available in the trade in question; and (c) that he presented a control card, filled in by the Principal of the High School, giving the period during which he had attended High School, before any benefits could be paid out.

It was required that the individual High Schools and recognized courses were on a special list, for benefits to be paid out. It was the responsibility of the Principal that the unemployed person would be able to gain a reasonable return from a term at High School, even if this had to be interrupted, and that he was accepted as a pupil on the same footing and for the same fees as the other pupils. This arrangement was later extended.

In addition to daily benefits, State and Local Authority aid was given on the usual conditions.

The number of unemployed entitled to daily benefits, in percentages of the total number of »year's pupils« at long and short courses, is shown in the following table:

	Number Unemployed	»Year's Pupils«	Total »Year's Pupils«	Unemployed Percentage »Year's Pupils«
1974/75	956	308	5077	5.9%
1975/76	1823	577	5180	11.1%
1976/77	2217	705	5089	13.8%
1977/78	2543	802	5498	14.6%

In the High Schools' total number of pupils, in addition to the number of actual »unemployed young persons« entitled to daily benefits, High School pupils are included who were not members of a trade union, and therefore not entitled to daily benefits. There were many of them. In many instances, these pupils had received assistance for a High School term through the local Social and Health Services. The number of such pupils has also increased considerably.

Out of the pupils entitled to daily benefits in 1976/77 and 1977/78, about 40% were over 25 years of age. Even though these were not all interested in a High School term, press comments showed that for most of them these terms came as a pleasant surprise. They found more zest in living. In the old days, the High Schools gave the farmers' sons self-confidence vis-à-vis the ruling classes. It was still their purpose to strengthen their pupils' grounds for self-confidence, even though the challenge was now of quite a different kind.

For young people threatened with unemployment, a local council could start a Production High School, giving both general information and practical training.

The Language High School on Kalø. Danish class for foreign students.

A glimpse of a class in folk dancing at the Gymnastics High School at Viborg.

Vestbirk High School. A music class.

Normal and handicapped pupils at Egmont High School.

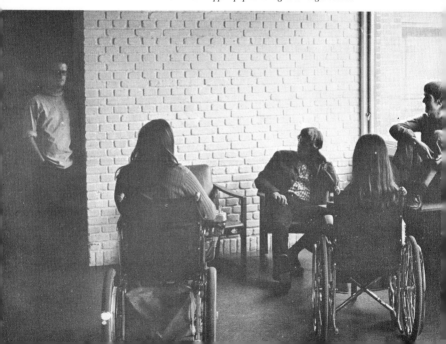

Happy gymnasts at the Gymnastics High School at Viborg.

Singing – acting – movement. Ærø Folk High School.

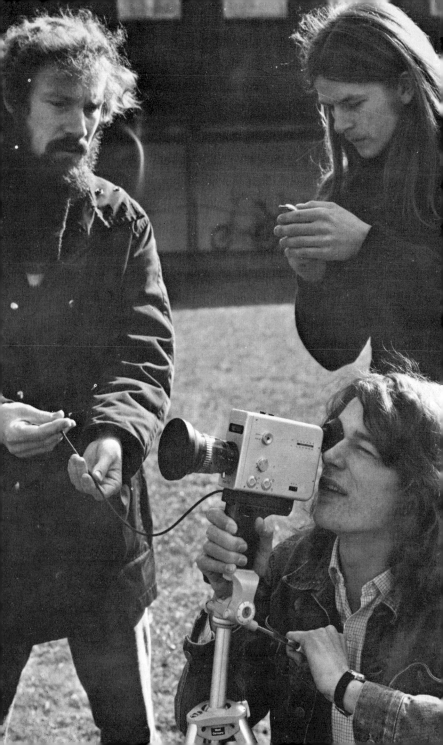

The High School Pupils' Own Opinion

»I became friends with myself.« With these words a former High School pupil summed up the benefit of his time at a High School, in a farewell letter after he had left the school. Many others have certainly had the same experience. The following excerpt from an article in the High School Paper of 5 January 1979 was written by a pupil at Sønderborg Physical Training High School in the winter of 1978/79:

»The High School more relevant than ever
»My opinion is that the mutual relationship where people are forced to live and work together, but at the same time need each other's support, gives an atmosphere of friendship and tolerance which one could wish was more general in society as a whole.

»The form of positive attitude to functioning collectively, which is encouraged at a High School, can be needed in high degree in later life. If people are not able to work in a community, problems can arise in a number of situations, which can be of vital importance both for the individual and for society.

»From the social point of view, it is considered useful if people learn that things 'have to be' done, even if it is hard. At a High School, as in other places, there can often be certain problems which are difficult, but the awareness that there is no one but ourselves to solve them gives greater personal flexibility than I have experienced previously. Both at primary and secondary school, one used to leave possible conflicts to the teacher or the headmaster, and as a rule one was not informed of the various problems, if they did not concern one personally.

»One feels clearly that the High School situation is more like the situation in society as a whole than the life one led in the school world.

»I do not think one can abolish the examination form in the educational system, but it is a fact that it gives one a pleasant freedom to work with things which interest one, if one is free from working on a comparatively fixed syllabus.

»The group working form also gives better conditions at a High School than in the rest of the educational system, because there one is usually examined in the same subject matter, and therefore must have been through the whole syllabus, whilst at a High School one can work on the special side of a problem which interests one, regardless of whether there are 2 or 10 who are interested in exactly the same field.

»Society's development has a tendency towards increasing alienation, both in one's job and in relation to others. Every effort must be made to stop this development with all means, and I believe that the High School can be a stage in this. At a High School, one is forced to have concern for each other, which means that one finds out that it is infinitely positive to be close to other people, both physically and psychologically.

»The very close contact under which we live is positive in the sense that one is educated to accept people's variety, but it also shows the enormous values there are in knowing that one can also get help from others. In modern industrialized

skov High School. Filming.

society, one often has the experience that people isolate themselves very much, and are afraid of showing their inner feelings. When this fear is spread among many people, a destructive alienation takes place, which in the long run can be a strong contributing cause of demoralization in our society.

»Naturally, the High School system cannot save society, but from what I have experienced of the High School environment, I believe that the High Schools can make their contribution together with a number of other factors.

»When I wish to save our society, it is not that I think that our society is good enough as it is today, but I believe that the High School contains a number of features which make it an important factor in many people's lives.

»One sees new High Schools springing up in many places, often with a more or less fixed political aim. This shows that there are many – also progressive forces – who have realised that the High School is a form under which things can be achieved which cannot be achieved under other forms.«

From the following little travesty, written by two pupils at Rødding High School shortly before the end of the winter term in 1978/79, one gets an impression of the fear of the future among a number of the 1970's unemployed High School youth:

The Future

(Melody: The Song about Larsen)

We came to school one day in November
and forgot about problems for a while.
But these days will soon be over and done
and the problems are turning up again.
It should be so good but it's really a mess.

Perhaps we shall end as unemployed,
have to stand in a queue for a stamp each day.
Here in Denmark are many who look for jobs
but we almost know what the answer'll be.
It should be so good but it's really a mess.

Or we'll end in a factory's grey routine,
a conveyor belt, and get a bad back,
or 4 buttons to push on our right-hand side,
a red, a yellow, a blue then a black.
It should be so good but it's really a mess.

If you're lucky you'll come to learn a trade
in a bank or maybe in an office.
Don't lose heart, though you've nearly lost hope.
They'll probably need us one fine day.
It should be so good but it's really a mess.

IX.

LEGISLATION AND ADMINISTRATIVE PRACTICE

The Various Forms of High School

The Folk High Schools in Denmark have acquired a unique position in that the State supports them without interfering in their affairs.

It was only a few years after Rødding High School was founded that the State began to give support to the running of the High Schools. The first grant was included in the Budget for 1851/52, with 2000 *rigsdaler* for »the peasant schools«. Annual subsidies were granted thereafter. The first Act granting aid to the High Schools was passed on 12 April 1892. This included the Agricultural Schools in the same subsidies. The law has been revised several times since then, for example in the Act of 29 April 1913 on State aid for High Schools and Agricultural Schools, and the Act of 4 July 1942 on High Schools and Agricultural Schools, which was superseded by the Act of 29 April 1955. The rules in force at present are contained in the Act of 4 June 1970 on Folk High Schools, Agricultural Schools, Domestic Science Schools and Continuation Schools.

The Act of 1942 did no more than the earlier subsidy laws to define the term »Folk High School«. It simply made it a condition for State aid that it should be a boarding school, with the requisite and properly furnished accommodation, so that the pupils usually lived on the premises during the school term. *Borup's High School* was the only exception. It was recognized as a day school covered by the High School Act. The law was based on the historically established idea that a Folk High School is an all-round educative school for young adults. It does not aim at examinations or technical training for use in business life.

It has always been accepted that High Schools are schools – not recreation centres. This means that there is work to be done.

But there are differences in the background, viewpoints, form and method of the individual High Schools. Some High Schools attach great importance to technical instruction. It has often been difficult for the Ministry to decide whether a school was a technical High School or a purely technical school, the recognition of which would blur the designation »Folk High School«. Earlier, many High Schools organised agricultural departments, artisan departments, domestic science departments, gymnastics departments or other technical departments. From the 1920's, Technical High Schools were also recognized as entitled to aid, provided the technical department was a secondary part of the whole plan of instruction. The pupils could receive aid as High School pupils, but they could not receive it if the technical department was predominant, and in that case they were not included in the numbers of High School pupils for the year.

In order to prevent the demarcation line between Folk High Schools and Technical Schools from being obliterated, the law of 1942 differentiated clearly between Folk High Schools, which place the main weight on all-round education, and Technical High Schools which give a single subject a predominant position. It also established that technical departments could be attached to Folk High Schools, but that Technical High Schools and technical departments were not allowed to prepare for examinations or entry to a school with an examination system. The Ministry of Education could give dispensation, however, and the distinction had no practical importance, since no differentiation was made in other provisions of the Act, between the two types of schools. It was not maintained, therefore, in the Act of 1970, which clearly defines the aims and activities of the High Schools:

§ 1, part 1. The Folk High School offers adult pupils general education and can within this give certain subjects or groups of subjects a prominent position.

§ 1, part 2. Where special conditions demand it, the Folk High Schools can offer teaching which gives recognized qualifications according to the rules laid down by the Ministry of Education.

148

The definition of what *general* education is, will vary considerably according to whether the school in question is to the right or the left of the Home Mission or a Tvind school. A High School is entitled to State aid, even if it aims at overthrowing the system, but this fact should be made clear in the clauses defining its aims or in its time table. The Ministry of Education can only intervene where insistence upon a certain attitude can lead to psychological violation of the pupils. – Some schools have language sides, music, art, social science sides, etc., training as gymnastics instructors, handicrafts teachers, woodwork teachers, preparatory courses for nursing or social service training. Two High Schools give courses for handicapped pupils which lead up to a final test. There are a number of intermediary types between the normal and technical preparatory High Schools. The decisive factor is that the High Schools attach importance to creating an environment for conversation and debate on existential or other cultural subjects.

Under the earlier law on the training of teachers, some High Schools had received permission to hold preparatory courses for prospective teachers college students. This arrangement was brought to an end in the new Act on the training of teachers, which made a matriculation examination or a higher preparatory examination obligatory for entrance to the teachers colleges. Under the provisions of the 1970 Act, §1, part 2, some High Schools received approval for holding technical preparatory examinations. Where the Ministry makes use of this avenue for dispensation, the qualifying instruction, which finishes with a test, must only take up a minor part of the courses.

A High School has no obligation to make reports on pupils, but it usually does so on request. This can help a pupil seeking admittance to a higher preparatory course, a recreation or kindergarten teachers training college, as a High School course of a certain duration is taken into account in evaluating a pupil's suitability for an advanced course. At a number of other educational institutions, some weight is attached to the student having attended a High School before entering the institution. This can also be the case as regards employment in private firms.

Many foreigners have been surprised that in Denmark private schools without syllabus or examinations can be financed with public funds. But it is in just this way that the State has guaranteed the Grundtvigian tradition of freedom and the independence of the Folk High Schools. In the 1970's, State aid constituted 50–60% of the income of most Folk High Schools. Added to this there are the individual grants to pupils, which will be dealt with later. Among the private schools, the High Schools received particularly favourable treatment. In 1976/77, the public contributions per year per pupil amounted to 18,830 kr. for Continuation Schools 17,074 kr. for Domestic Science Schools, 19,922 kr. for Agricultural Schools and 22,030 kr. for Folk High Schools.

As a condition for State aid to a newly established High School, the Act of 1892 demanded that the High School should be included in the Budget, the Ministry of Education having already approved the syllabus. This meant that for a trial period of one year the school had had at least 10 »year's pupils« (see p. 104). This trial period was extended under a later law, and the State aid was discontinued if a school had not had an average of 5 »year's pupils« for 3 years. The Act of 1942 determined that the approval of a new High School could be given on a purely administrative basis, but it was conditional on a particular person being the Principal. This meant that, formally speaking, a school did not exist from the moment a Principal retired until a new Principal was appointed. Approval was the only condition for the school to be able to receive State-aided pupils.

The Act of 1970, like the previous Acts, established that a High School must be equipped as a boarding school, but that it can also accept pupils living at home, who take part in its day-to-day activities. The law does not rule out the possibility, in certain cases – for example in large densely built-up areas – for High Schools to be established without dormitory facilities for the pupils. But in the appendix to the proposal for the Act it is emphasized that such a day school must not only offer education, but also meals and recreational activities, so that the comradeship between pupils and teachers, which is a characteristic feature of the boarding school form, can be fully developed.

Approval of a High School is announced by the Minister of Education on the following conditions:

1. The school shall be a private, self-governing institution, the rules of which have been approved by the Minister of Education. According to the provisions of the earlier Education Acts, it was also a condition for approval of a State loan to start a new school or enlarge an existing High School, that the school in question was a self-governing institution, and State loans could be granted for the conversion of a school into a self-governing institution. Only two High Schools had not made use of this offer, when the Act of 1970 came into force.

2. The Principal of the school shall be approved by the Minister of Education. Hereafter, the school and the principal can no longer be identified direct, since the approval of the principal is now only one of the conditions which must be met for the school to be approved as such. The approval of a principal still rests on an evaluation of his professional qualifications, teaching experience and expectations as to his successful leadership of the school's work.

3. The school shall have suitable premises at its disposal and the requisite equipment. This rule establishes by law the practice followed in the other types of free schools, where, at the time of approval, stress was laid upon suitable accommodation being available.

4. The school curriculum shall be approved by the Minister of Education. The earlier laws did not demand approval of the curriculum, but it was an administrative demand that a curriculum of the school courses should be approved both at the start of the school and if the courses were later altered.

Approval can be withdrawn from a school, if it no longer fulfils the conditions mentioned above, or if its teaching or other circumstances are in evident disharmony with the directives generally followed by Folk High Schools: for example, if, after a school has been running for some time, it proves that the teaching is not up to such a standard as to create an educational environment for its pupils, or if the external framework or the meals are unsatisfactory.

From 1876, the Ministry of Education had a salaried inspector for the High Schools, but in the Act of 1942 provision was made for the position of State Consultant for young adult education, on a Civil Service basis, to be responsible for inspection of Folk High Schools and Agricultural Schools. Later, the Director of Primary and Lower Secondary Education, Youth and Adult Education, Teacher Training, etc. became Inspector under the Minister of Education.

The Act of 1942 laid down that to obtain State aid, a Folk High School must have carried out one course of at least 5 months' duration or 2 courses of 3 months' duration, during the previous financial year. Corresponding to this, the Act of 1970 lays down that the school must have carried out one approved course of at least 20 weeks' duration, or 2 approved courses of at least 12 weeks' duration. Attendance is required of an average of at least 18 »year's pupils« during the previous 3 financial years (corresponding to 15 »year's pupils« according to the previous calculation, as the number of »year's pupils« is no longer calculated by dividing the total number of pupils per month by 12, but by dividing the total number of pupils per week by 40).

For a full school year, at least 32 weeks of approved teaching is required, corresponding to the 8 months laid down in the earlier law. If a school is not used to capacity with courses of this length, a proportionate reduction is carried out in the calculation of the State aid, depending upon the number of pupils for the year. The expenses, for which these contributions are made consist of (1) maintenance of the buildings, (2) taxes, dues, etc., (3) hire of rooms and land, (4) interest on loans against mortgages on the buildings, and (5) fees for auditors, secretaries and caretakers.

In addition, it is a condition for aid that the Principal of the school and the teachers receive salaries according to the rules laid down by the Minister of Education. The terms of appointment of the other members of the staff shall be agreed in writing.

Principals and Teachers

Earlier, as mentioned previously, it was usually the principal who ran the school at his own expense and risk, whether he owned it himself or leased it through a circle of friends of the school. As approval was attached to the person of the principal, and was withdrawn on a change of principal, he dismissed his whole staff when he resigned, so that the new principal would have a free hand in his choice of teachers. Teachers were often re-appointed by the new principal, but there were just as many examples of their having to seek other employment. Their position was thus very insecure, so that it could often be difficult to find qualified candidates for vacant positions. The work was comprehensive and very demanding, also after school hours, particularly at the small, home-like High Schools, with a patriarchal principal, where there was no institutional atmosphere. There was little time for the teacher's private life. As an example of what a High School teacher had to live up to, a letter of appointment from 1947 is given below, with the conditions which a principal could lay down at that time:

»The duties of the appointment are as follows: A weekly programme of between 20 and 25 hours, of which from 6 to 12 are lecture hours, must be covered. He takes part, with the Principal, in leading and arranging all parties and meetings and in being responsible for all matters concerning repairs of premises and material. He must be willing to see to telephoning workmen and suppliers. He has the duty of daily supervision of pupils, pupils' rooms and school classrooms, also including checking the pupils' punctual return after Sunday and holiday leave, and of their punctual use of heating, light, water and gymnastics equipment etc. He is obliged, except on his weekly free day and free evening, both on Sundays and weekdays to be present at all school meals, and his wife and children are also normally expected to take part in these, with the exception of breakfast.

»It must be stressed particularly that he, like the Principal and other teachers, must consider it as an essential part of his duties to keep his home open both to present and past pupils, both singly and in groups. It goes without saying that the demands of his private life and his work will be somewhat limited by this, but no reservation can be made in any of the following three requirements:

1) On Sundays, and particularly on Sunday evenings, he and his wife and his home must always be at the disposal of the pupils. They must take it as a matter of course that they receive their visits for one or two hours, or meet them in the school building, they must also be prepared to give part of the day to gatherings

and arrangements for their entertainment, and this must take priority over or be combined with meeting private guests. The weekly free day is provided for this reason, and the teacher or teacher's wife who is not willing to bring this sacrifice to the work should not apply for the position.

2) On at least two of the other evenings of the week, some time should be reserved for receiving short visits from pupils and talking with them.

3) Their doors must be open to a considerable extent for old pupils visiting the school. Cultivating relationships with these is an especially important part of the work.«

The special importance of the principal's functions was repeated in the charter of the self-governing institutions which the High Schools established in the first years after 1942, as the provisions assign the responsibility for the running of the school and the responsibility for the teaching to the principal. He was to appoint and dismiss teachers, possibly in consultation with the Board of Directors; and within the limits of the law on salaries, he had a free hand in these appointments. He had the over-riding authority to decide in which salary grades the individual teacher should be placed, unless the provisions clearly stated otherwise, and it was exceptional for these to contain provisions on the teachers councils and the pupils councils.

Later Rules

In 1959, a majority in the Association of High Schools and Agricultural Schools agreed to publish the pamphlet *The High School Teachers' Position,* of which the revised edition of 1965 contained a decision on teachers councils. But the little pamphlet did not quote the provisions of the Act direct, and consisted only of guidance. It was not unimportant, however, and after a time, several schools obtained co-operative organs which brought staff and pupils into joint responsibility for the running of the school.

It was not until the Act of 1970 that it was laid down that principals and teachers should form teachers councils. According to the *High School Teachers' Position* (edition of 1979), all questions regarding school work should be dealt with in the teachers council, including (a) establishment of courses and length of courses, (b) preparation of teaching programme and time table, (c) planning of new building and alteration projects, (d) major purchases of teaching material and books, (e) preparation and administration of the school regulations. In addition, the teachers council shall have the opportunity to express its opinions when teachers or principals are dismissed, and if the school charters are altered, and the schools' statements of account and budgets shall be presented every year at a meeting of the teachers council.

Where these rules are followed, the sole authority of the principal has been greatly diminished. But since the Act contains no mention of the rights of teachers councils, there are considerable differences between the various High Schools. Legally, however, the function of the principal is simply to represent the school *vis-à-vis* the Minister of Education. It is no longer a condition that he be appointed for an indefinite period. There are schools where the charters include rules on appointments for limited periods. Some High Schools are run collectively, in reality, even if not from a legal point of view, since the Ministry only approves one person as principal. When a change of principal occurs, schools must apply for approval of a new principal, as soon as possible. If necessary, a principal can be constituted. But the appointment of teachers is not affected as it was previously by a change of principal.

Principals are appointed and dismissed by the Board of Directors and/or the General Assembly, according to the stipulations of the regulations. From these it will also be clear that the principal alone and/or in consultation with the executive board appoints and dismisses teachers. There must be a written contract between the school and the individual teacher on the form of appointment, payment for lodging, board and other payments in kind, as well as the rules regarding dismissal. The teacher's grading as regards salary is no longer decided by the principal, or by him in consultation with the Board of Directors, but by the Ministry, on the basis of a questionnaire regarding grading filled in by the teacher.

A teacher on the permanent staff must give 600 hours of

teaching a year, but he may be allowed to take on more hours, without extra payment, and take part in arranging and running excursions and amateur theatricals, gymnastics and physical training displays etc., or take charge of the school collections and teaching material, etc. He must be able to deputize for the principal for short periods, and he also has the duty, if the school so wishes, to take part in, or possibly be in charge of a daily common meal. For these reasons, the number of teaching hours is comparatively low.

State Aid to High Schools

According to the Act of 1892, every school received a modest direct State grant in advance, for each »year's pupil«, up to one-third of the cost of the teachers' salaries and teaching material, within a fixed maximum amount.

The Act of 1913 differentiated between the following forms of subsidized running costs:

A. The basis subsidy of 500 kr. This was increased to 1000 kr. under the law of 1942, and later to 2–4,000 kr., the size of the subsidies being in reverse proportion to the number of pupils per year, in consideration of the small schools.
B. The building subsidy of 0.6% of the valuation of the school buildings. In the Act of 1942, this was increased to 2%, and later to $3^{1}/_{2}$%.
C. The subsidy for teachers' salaries of 50%. Later a maximum amount was stipulated for subsidized teachers' salaries, and in 1942 also a minimum. In the Act of 1955, the grant was increased to 70%.
D. The subsidy towards the principal's salary, of 20% of his salary as a teacher. This was abolished in 1942, but reinstated a few years later. In 1955, it was increased to 70%, if the school was a self-governing institution.
E. The subsidy for teaching material of 35% of the purchase sum. In 1955 it was increased to 50%.

156

From 1942, in addition to the subsidy towards running costs, a further amount was provided by the State as a seniority supplement for the individual principals and teachers, rising after 5, 10 and 15 years' seniority. In the Act of 1892, a yearly sum had already been made available to the Ministry of Education, for individual schools where the activities and conditions particularly recommended it. This amounted to 10,000 kr. in all.

According to the Act of 18 June 1969 on State aid for certain private schools, the State aid amounts to 85% of the following costs:

A. Salaries of principals and teachers.
B. Maintenance of the school buildings.
C. Heating, lighting and cleaning of the buildings, and electricity and water supplies.
D. Taxes, dues, and insurance premiums in regard to the buildings.
E. Lease of premises and land.
F. Interest and loans against mortgages on the school property.
G. Other expenses in connexion with the running of the school.

The subsidy for principals' and teachers' salaries is limited to 85 hours per »year's pupil«. The ceiling for the maintenance costs is fixed at $2^{1}/_{2}\%$ of the valuation of the buildings. A limit is also set for the subsidy for the actual expenses under §C. This is fixed in relation to the number of »year's pupils« multiplied by the average payments per pupil in the State schools which are not used for other purposes than the running of the school. The rent for leasing premises (such as a school kitchen) and land (for example for playing-fields), like the loan against mortgages on school property, must be approved by the Minister of Education. Whilst the amounts in rent are included, within the limit, in the basic subsidy, the loans for which the interest is subsidized are subject to a limit set by the Minister of Education. The subsidy to other expenses (office staff, administration, etc.) is calculated according to the number of »year's pupils«.

Approved self-governing institutions, eligible for subsidies, can also be granted State loans for the erection or purchase of buildings and inventory, and for extension and improvements, etc., of existing schools. These loans can amount to 50% of the building or purchasing costs. Repayment of the loans is not required, and the interest is 4% p.a. It is a condition that plans and designs are approved by the Minister of Education, and that the institution itself has raised at least one-sixth of the building or purchase sum. The loan is secured by mortgage with the right to take the place of prior, obsolete mortgages, within five-sixths of the value of the property.

The above regulations mean that it is now easier to finance the start of new High Schools than it was under the Act of 1942, which demanded that the institution itself must raise an amount corresponding to one quarter of the value of the property.

In addition, a State loan can be made on the conditions mentioned, when building, major conversions, or improvements, including the acquisition of expensive equipment and teaching material, are needed to modernize a school.

Grants to Pupils

To obtain a State grant for a term at a High School, no demands are made in the Act, apart from the condition that the pupil shall be at least 17$^{1}/_{2}$ years of age at the beginning of the course. The individual school can demand a higher age, such as 19, 20 or 21, or choose its pupils from particular groups of society by making nurseries, kindergartens, etc. available. As regards pensioners courses, there is no age ceiling.

The law contains no provisions for possible co-operative organs, joint meetings with staff, pupils councils, etc. These questions, like the school regulations, are left entirely to the discretion of the particular school.

In the Act of 1892, an annual appropriation was made available by the Ministry of Finance for grants to students amounting to slightly over 60% of the monthly payment per pupil, for up to half the total of the pupils for the previous financial year. However, the total aid might not exceed a certain yearly maximum.

Following the Act of 1942, the Ministry of Education, on request of the Association of High Schools and Agricultural Schools, had to decide the amount estimated as necessary both to cover teaching and lodging, books and other necessary expenses for the term. The State aid could be granted for 70% of the amount fixed. The size of the grant to each pupil should be fixed on a points system, based on the pupil's and his or her parents' income and capital in the previous financial year. Each point corresponded to a particular percentage of aid, in such a way that the percentage figure fell as the points rose. Points were substracted in proportion to the number of the pupil's brothers and sisters under 14 years of age. Pupils over 24, however, and married, separated or divorced pupils, were evaluated on their own economic situation alone.

This arrangement was not altogether satisfactory, however. It meant that young people from modest homes received comparatively little support, whilst those from more well-to-do homes, who did not need to earn their living, often received considerable aid, because their own incomes were low. According to the present rules, the points system is maintained, but on somewhat different lines, so that it is given solely on the basis of the parents' or spouse's taxable income, and with a reduction in points for brothers and sisters or the pupil's own children under the age of 18. The economic situation of the parents is not taken into consideration where the candidate is 21 years of age and over, or married.

The payment for pupils can vary somewhat from one school to another, but the sums fixed by the Minister of Education for the expenses which constitute the basis of the aid (the framework of the pupils' grants) are the same for all schools, as before. It has been changed to include only payment for teaching and lodging, on request by the Association of Folk High Schools in Denmark. The State aid given consists of a sum from 10–70% of the approved weekly expenses, and it is only given to participants in courses of at least 2 weeks' duration. The local authorities have the right to give further aid to cover the remaining expenses for teaching and lodging. Lastly, the High School Fund gives aid for terms at a High School (p. 116).

159

X.

EFFECTS ON OTHER TYPES OF SCHOOL

Continuation Schools

The private Continuation School, which offers all-round schooling to youngsters between 14 and 18, is an especially Danish phenomenon, without any parallel in the other Nordic countries. Like the High Schools, it originates in the Grundtvig-Kold ideas on education, but the High Schools were the first to come to the fore. In the period between 1864 and 1890 new High Schools were constantly being established. There was less increase among the Continuation Schools. Nevertheless, the High School which Christen Kold started at Ryslinge Mark, and several of the other higher peasant schools, were in reality Continuation Schools, since the pupils were so young. Although Kold later realised that High School pupils must be older, he did not forget how important it was that schools should be available for young adolescents.

Added to this, a number of the free school teachers who were former pupils from Christen Kold's school were unwilling to drop the children when they reached Confirmation age. The idea of a continuation school was obvious, and in 1879 Kold's assistant teacher Povlsen-Dal started a Continuation School on Mors. In the period that followed, it was particularly on Funen that Continuation Schools appeared, attached to the Free Schools. At the end of their 7-year schooling, the 14 to 15-year-olds attended all-day or half-day school throughout one winter, but as a rule few or none of them lived at the school. They did not therefore form a school society together with the teachers. There is considerable evidence that the idea for the municipal youth schools, which were introduced in the law of

Uldum High School. Swimming class.

The Jutland Physical Training School. Open air swimming pool.

Askov High School. At the loom.

The Travelling High School. Preparations for an excursion.

Modern teaching methods, such as group work, are included in the Jutland Pensioners High School programme.

Good company at Herning High School.

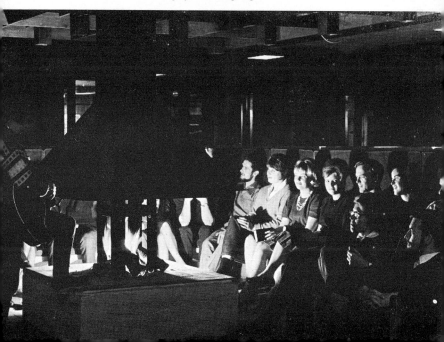

1942, was taken from the private continuation school education.

As late as in 1945, about one-third of the Continuation Schools were attached to the Kold Free Schools. They acknowledged their relationship to the High Schools, and more and more of them went over to the boarding school form, particularly the »frontier schools«, as they were called. Here the background was the Germanization of the North Slesvig schools, where after 1888 Danish was ruled out, except in scripture lessons. The »frontier schools« were: *Skibelund* (1874), *Hejls* (1876), *Holsted* (1892), *Vester Vedsted* (1895), *Bramminge* (1897), and *Skanderup* (1914). Young South Jutlanders came to these schools in order to meet Danish culture and home life. Their semesters were the same as those of the High Schools, with the boys in the winter and the girls in the summer. Later the well-known Northern Jutland Continuation Schools were started under the designation of »youth schools«. This was a form of school with more emphasis on practical training, but at the same time was built up on the tradition from the frontier schools.

In 1895, they obtained aid, allowed for in the Budget, on the condition that »they were of real use to the district where they were working«. Their numbers grew from 26 at the turn of the century to 57 in 1940. At the same time, the number of High Schools fell. Several of them were converted into Continuation Schools, such as *Nørre Ørslev* on Falster, *Sorø* and *Brøderup* on Zealand, *Særslev* and *Vejstrup* on Funen, and *Galtrup, Klank, Salling* and *Vivild* in Jutland. Hoptrup High School acquired a continuation school department in 1920. One or two other High Schools followed suit, but apart from these, all the Continuation Schools had their own separate premises.

Under the Act of 4 July 1942, those Continuation Schools which were self-governing institutions were placed on an equal footing with the High Schools as regards State aid. This, combined with better grants for the pupils, led to the establishment of many new Continuation Schools up to 1960, and increasing intake of pupils.

The increase in the numbers of pupils per year from 1965/66 is noteworthy. It has been due not only to the increased number

v High School. The Folk High School Song Book is often in use.

	Number of Continuation Schools	Number of Pupils	Continuation School Frequency[1]	Number of »Year's Pupils«[2]
1940/41	57	2756		
1945/46	65	3581		
1950/51	75	4535		
1955/56	91	6150		
1960/61	107	9982	12 %	
1965/66	103	7794	10 %	4579
1970/71	101	6922	9 %	6200
1975/76	112	8745	11 %	7942
1976/77	114	9056	12 %	8140
1977/78	113	10158	13 %	9091

1. Number of Continuation School pupils in percentages of 16 year-olds.
2. 40 weeks school year.

of pupils, but also to the fact that more and more Continuation Schools have introduced long courses of 40 weeks. Almost all Continuation Schools now have capacity for 30 to 140 pupils. The age of the pupils has risen somewhat. In 1976 it was 16½ years.

Continuation Schools can be approved by the Minister of Education, if the following conditions are met:

1. The school shall be a private self-governing institution, whose charter has been approved by the Minister of Education.
2. The principal of the school shall be approved by the Minister of Education.
3. The school shall have suitable premises at its disposal, and the requisite equipment.
4. The school's syllabus shall have been approved by the Minister of Education.

The majority of the Continuation Schools became co-educational. At the end of the 1960's they nearly all introduced the primary schools' State-controlled tests. They were no longer free from examinations and curricula, but could fulfil the obligatory teaching requirements for the 8th and 9th school years. The pupils could have a beneficial change of environment, and unlike the High School pupils, could obtain the same qualifications as in the primary schools. However, only about half of the Continuation School pupils were of compulsory school age. Some returned to the primary schools after their Continuation School term. Incidentally, many Continuation Schools preferred the designation »Youth Schools« (not to be confused with the municipal youth schools), and even if they showed a clear difference from the High Schools, in their form and content, for many young people they replaced the High Schools. It was more a question of »either or«, than »both and«, because the pupils could also experience the values of a boarding school, at a Continuation School.

The Grundtvig-Kold Free Schools

The designation »Free School« was originally given to folk schools which gave gratis teaching. It was not until the Education Act of 1814 was passed that all parents had the right of free schooling for their children. Later the »Free Schools« came to designate private paying schools, which shared Grundtvig's and Kold's educational ideas.

With Kold's educational activity in Dalby in 1852 as their model, the Free Schools laid the main emphasis on elementary teaching in arithmetic and Danish, and awakening to Christian and national life. The means to this awakening was free narrative, from the Bible and from the myths of the mother country's past.

The Act of 2 May 1855 allowed for private teaching and education at home, on condition that the children received education of the standard demanded at a primary school. Free Schools were started especially in the districts where Grundtvig revivalist movements had prepared the soil, particularly on Funen, in West Jutland, and on Mors. The teachers were often former High School pupils. In 1920, 252 Free Schools were grouped as follows, according to the year in which they were started:

1850–59	1860–69	1870–79	1880–89	1890–99	1900–09	1910–19	In all
14	49	72	49	25	27	16	252

The greatest increase in Free Schools was during »the great High School period«. But in some instances it was the poor conditions in the local primary schools, or disagreement between parents and a teacher that prompted the start of a Free School. One cannot see from the statistics how many of these Free Schools were later closed. After 1920, closures were more numerous than openings of new schools. Since 1970, however, there has been a noticeable increase in the numbers of pupils at the Grundtvig-Kold Free Schools. It may seem that the parents of children of school age have again understood the home-like character of this school form, and the importance of the small classes. In 1978, 96 schools with 8241 pupils (1st to 10th school year) were entered in the Danish Free School Union. The size of the school in relation to the number of pupils was as follows:

Number of pupils at schools	0–20	21–40	41–60	61–80	81–120	121–160	161–200	over 200
Number of schools	7	23	11	19	14	13	3	6

The 7-year schooling could be extended with 8th to 10th school years, according to the provisions of the Primary School Act. The pupils had the right of examination at the end of the 9th and 10th form, and the Free Schools had the duty to arrange that the examinations were held. The State gives considerable aid to the Free Schools which are self-governing institutions, and grants to pupils. The parents association chooses a local inspector, who must be approved by the Minister of Education. This inspector may not be one of the parents.

164

The reaction against the large schools also led to circles of parents starting so-called Little Schools. These Free Schools, however, were not based on the Grundtvig-Kold view of life.

The Free Teachers College

Like Krogerup High School and Båring High School, *The Free Teachers College* in Ollerup belonged to the group of folk initiatives, which were inspired by the folk fellowship of the Occupation.

On the background of the realisation that the Grundtvig-Kold educational ideas should be reflected in the training of teachers, if they were to survive, a college had been started in Elbæk with a 2-year course without examinations, for the training of teachers for the Free Schools; but time was short and the demands all the greater, however much good will there was. It was therefore considered inadequate to have only one teachers college (which actually survived for a number of years). In 1943, the Askov teacher, Holger Kjær, advocated the establishment of a new examination-free teachers college, attached to a free Nordic Teachers High School. At about the same time, the High School Principal Ejnar Skovrup, Kerteminde, presented a fully prepared plan, and in 1944 he started the *Free Danish Teachers College* at *Kerteminde High School*. He had to give up, however, for private reasons. Together with 3 teacher families, the pupils moved to *Vestbirk High School*, where they waited to hear to what extent they would have the possibility of continuing and finishing their teachers training.

In this situation, a committee of interested High School and Free School folk found it was reasonable to carry on with the teachers college in another location, and in 1949 they bought *Ollerup High School*. Owing to lack of funds, the idea was that the traditional High School pupils should be able to use the school's vacant capacity, until a 4-year teacher training had been built up.

The school began its first term on 15 September the same year, with 2 small classes of former pupils from Vestbirk and a

165

large new class of first year pupils. The work had to be done in the most modest conditions, as the school gave technical training and therefore could not obtain State allowances within the framework of the High School Act, and was not a recognized Teachers College. The then Principal Jørgen Bøgh wrote on that difficult period:

»One could expect assistants, pupils and oneself to put up with conditions which would have emptied any school, today. No one really minded whether there was money for salaries – whether the food was more solid than exciting, and a successful cabbage harvest made itself felt at dinner for a whole winter – whether the beds dated from an age when 175 cm was a proper length – whether several people had to share a room and the sanitary installations were always on the point of collapse – whether even in the late night hours or at cock crow one had to listen to one finger music exercises, because there were too few instruments for the compulsory music instruction and practice during the day time – and whether the biology collection was identical with the natural life to be found in the school garden . . . (But) friendship and solidarity between pupils, teachers and personnel came to leave its mark on the first years, where we struggled with a bottomless economy and uncertainty as regards the recognition of the school in the educational system.«

According to the provisions of the first foundation, the school should not only train teachers for Free Schools, Continuation Schools and High Schools, but also for the Primary Schools. The principle, not to hold examinations, was questioned several times. The first time was in 1952, because the pupils could not be accepted for teaching positions in the Primary Schools. But while Jørgen Bøgh wished to introduce examinations, because he was afraid that the Free Schools could not absorb the coming teachers from Ollerup, others, and particularly the pupils themselves, stood firm in the faith, and examinations are still unthinkable. In 1953, Bøgh was replaced as Principal by Harald Bredsdorff, who was in turn replaced by Vilhelm Nielsen, the later Inspector of Education. In 1972, Flemming Trænæs became Principal.

Up to 1959, normal High School education still continued parallel with teacher training, but it had to be abandoned owing to diminishing intake, and Ollerup High School changed its name to *The Free Teachers College*. The provisions of the foundation from 1970 read in part, »the purpose of the school is to train teachers primarily for Free Schools, Continuation Schools and High Schools, but also for other school forms, as well as to be leaders of the folk youth work. The school does not prepare pupils for any examinations.« A possibility is open for a school leaver to take a supplementary test in Danish, arithmetic, the pedagogical subjects and a special subject. He is then qualified to teach in a Primary and Lower Secondary School. Few have taken advantage of this offer, and on grounds of principle, the tests cannot be taken at the Free Teachers College itself.

Unlike the Teacher Training Colleges with examinations, the Free Teachers College insists on compulsory attendance at classes. These are prepared, as to content and method, by the individual teacher and the pupils together. No definite syllabus is required, since the main emphasis is laid upon motivation. There is simply a certain framework which must be approved by the Minister for allocations to be granted. The teachers therefore have considerable pedagogic freedom, but they also have a heavy responsibility as regards choice of material and teaching methods. The teachers' calling therefore resembles that of the High School teachers in many ways, more than the ordinary Teacher Training College trainees'. It is essential that the pupils can live up to the particular responsibility implicit in attending a non-examination school.

In 1965 the training course was extended to 5 years, with plenty of time for practice, both with and without actual teaching work at a school. The Teachers College takes 45 pupils every year. In the first period the college was attended particularly by »the man from the plough« and »the girl from the kitchen«, but in later years pupils have come with quite different backgrounds, such as a job in town. The matriculation examination or the higher preparatory examination is not a condition for acceptance. The candidate must simply have an education corresponding to 10 years' schooling with the tests involved, be at least 20 years of age, and have acquired some practical knowledge of life outside the school world. The school provides board and residence. As at the High Schools, such an environment permits the closest co-operation between the pupils themselves and between teachers and pupils, after the actual teaching hours. At the end of the course, the pupils receive school-leaving certificates with the teachers' remarks on proficiency in the various subjects.

The Free Teachers College, after some rough seas, has entered calm waters. It represents an important achievement for the Grundtvig educational concepts, and at the same time it is in harmony with modern education. Several of the High School Principals in the country are former students from the Free Teachers College.

The Agricultural Schools

A foreigner visiting an Agricultural School, who is already familiar with the Folk High School, will find many similarities between the two school forms, except for the natural difference in subjects. Both are boarding schools, where pupils share the simple daily life with the teachers.

With the exception of *The Classen Farming School* at Næsgaard (Falster), which was started in 1849, the Agricultural Schools, in their democratic form, go back to 1867, with *Lyngby Farming School*. Its founder, Jørgen la Cour, once stated: »The Danish Farming School is a child of the Danish Folk High School«. For la Cour it was essential to combine the High School and Agricultural School education under one roof. In its first year, the school had a High School course from October to April, and an agricultural course from October to August. A High School course was a necessary condition for acceptance to the agricultural department, but here too there were general educative High School subjects on the time table. Teaching was given in history, Danish, singing, geographical description (particularly of the nature and national ways of life under foreign skies), arithmetic, writing, drawing and physical training. This was in keeping with the fact that before 1864, the Peasant High Schools were both High Schools and Agricultural Schools.

The years 1867–79 were the Farming Schools' period. Lyngby Farming School was the model for the agricultural department which was opened in 1869 at *Hindholm High School*, with a course of 9 months for pupils who had already attended High School. In 1871, their leaders took over Michael Gjøe's High School in Tune, which they converted into *Tune Farming School*. Like Lyngby Farming School, it also had a High School department as a preparatory school to the Agricultural department, and here, too, there were High School subjects in the agricultural department: 3 weekly lectures on myths, legends and sagas, 3 on Danish history and 3 on world history. In addition, 3 hours of physics and 6 of gymnastics, and every evening one hour of literary readings. In 1891, the High School department had to close, but in the School's jubilee publication of 1946, it is stated that in the period thereafter, efforts were continued, to »satisfy the need for experience of a spiritual kind, which the pupils brought with them, as well as their need for technical training«.

With the start of *Ladelund Agricultural School* in 1879, the real era of the Agricultural School began. In spite of the limited duration of the courses – 5 months – a good deal of the High School teaching was included. The aim of the school was not only to give useful information and knowledge. This was also true of *Dalum Agricultural School,* which came in 1886, although at the meeting to consider establishing the school, its principal had made a point of giving everyone to understand that it was to be a purely technical school. The pupils received a solid orientation on national and social questions, and social economy. The teaching at *Malling Agricultural School* (1889) was of a more technical nature, as at many of the Agricultural Schools which were started after the turn of the century. The old Farming Schools also gave more room for technical instruction in agricultural subjects.

With the structural changes in 1945, and especially after the Act of 1970, the High Schools and the Agricultural Schools grew away from each other.

The *Horticultural Schools*, like the former *Small-holders' Schools*, were recognized on a line with the Agricultural Schools, and included general subjects. Among these, the *Gardeners' and Fruit Farmers' School*, »Søhus« near Odense, has also been approved as a High School, since 1975.

The High Schools and Agricultural Schools have adjusted

themselves in their respective ways to the structural changes and the technical-economic developments. In 1971, the *Association of High Schools and Agricultural Schools* was changed to the *Association of Folk High Schools in Denmark*, without the membership of the Agricultural Schools.

Domestic Science Schools and Artisan Schools

The Domestic Science Schools, like the Folk High Schools, Agricultural Schools and Continuation Schools, belong to the group of institutions designated as Free Schools.

The first Domestic Science School was started in Sorø in 1895. Later it became a Domestic Science teachers school. The founder's close ties with Askov High School resulted in its becoming a technical school with a High School climate. Like *Sorø Domestic Science School*, »Ankerhus«, the other Domestic Science Schools which were started in the period that followed, were based on the Folk High School concept, with the »living word« in teaching, and an understanding of the importance of comradeship in daily life between teachers and pupils.

Nearly all Domestic Science Schools are boarding schools. They are a combination between general educative and business oriented teaching, related particularly to the home and family. In later years, special emphasis has been placed on teaching pupils to administer the work in a home where both husband and wife have jobs. Many Domestic Science Schools also provide instruction in gymnastics, foreign languages and literature.

Like the Domestic Science Schools, the Artisan Schools have traditional ties to the Folk High Schools. In 1877, Ernst Trier started an artisan department at Vallekilde High School. It was soon well attended.

Artisan departments were gradually established in several other High Schools, with Vallekilde as their model. At the turn of the century, 16 High Schools had established artisan departments. In the years up to 1914, 10 more High Schools started artisan departments, but at the same time, some of the other High Schools closed their artisan departments.

There were High School folk who were in doubt as regards artisan departments. They found that the lecture work and Danish lessons were neglected because the pupils' time was taken up with all the work connected with purely technical reading matter. To avoid trouble with the High School folk, a demand came from the artisans for independent Artisan Schools, where the pupils lived and had their meals as at High Schools.

The first Artisan School, the *Builders, Carpenters and Painters School in Holbæk,* was started in 1915. In 1922, the artisan department of the Home Mission High School in Haslev broke away and became independent, under the name *Haslev Artisan School.* The same year, the artisan department of Hadsten High School was converted into *Hadsten Artisan School.* In 1939, the *Artisan School Sønderborg Technical School* was started. These schools all had a strongly technical character, and were not administered under the High School law. The situation was somewhat different at *Brandbjerg High School,* which was started in 1951 as a Folk High School for artisans, but which has later admitted pupils from all sectors of the population.

Evening High Schools

After the War, the High Schools' enlightenment work found new channels via the evening schools, as the Act of 4 July 1942, and the Occupation encouraged instruction which could take place in the Evening High School. It drew attendance from circles far wider than those of the traditional High Schools.

The Evening High School was one of the results of the work of the Youth Commission set up in 1939. A member of the commission, Jens Rosenkjær, came out strongly in favour of schooling in which young people could take part without having to give up their jobs. He took the initiative in getting possibilities opened up for the start of Evening High Schools, to stimulate interest in civic and cultural subjects, with study circles and lectures as the most important forms of teaching. A modest allowance could be obtained for the purchase of educational material, and grants for foreign lecturers. A revision of the law in 1954 brought no major changes in the rules for aid. The Evening High School had passed its test. It had become a cultural centre in towns and parishes.

According to the Act of 6 June 1968 on Leisure-time Education, etc., with later revisions, Evening High Schools and lecture series with humanist, sociological and natural science subjects could be recognized as eligible for aid. The teaching, which must not have technical or practical objectives, must be available for anyone over 18 years of age, and it must not lead up to a final test or examination. A lecture series must only include one group of subjects, and must consist of at least 4 lectures. It must start with at least 25 participants. In thinly populated areas, however, the number of participants can be reduced to 15. The lectures must be approved before the lecture series begin, and they must be carried out according to plan. The State and Local Authority each gives aid amounting to $^3/_8$ of the expenses for fees and payment per hour, to the Evening High School. For the lecture series the State gives aid amounting to $^1/_3$ of the fees up to a certain maximum.

In addition to the Local Authority, the political organisations and many private associations have started Evening High Schools and lecture series within the framework of the law. One finds High School teachers, clergymen, lawyers, doctors, gymnastics instructors, industrial workers and farmers among the study circle leaders and lecturers. They enjoy considerable freedom in their choice of material. Since the High School has been the source of inspiration, in many places the lecture form has been chosen, with its close contact between lecturer and participants. In the towns there is a preference for study circles. Both in town and country importance is attached to the interchange of ideas on society and human life, the significance of which Grundtvig stressed so strongly in his writings on the High School. In addition to the questions of socially oriented character, the history of art, psychology and Danish literature have met great interest in the Evening High Schools, whilst many lecture series have been concerned with purely human problems, literary subjects or with Danish and foreign political questions.

The High Schools in the other Nordic Countries

The Grundtvig High School ideas have also had practical effect in the rest of Scandinavia, although the Norwegian, Swedish and Finnish High Schools each retain their national character. However, there can be striking differences between the High Schools of a single country, because of the freedom which the High School Act gives them. The High School world guarded this freedom, especially in Denmark, as regards the organisation of the schools and the length and content of the courses. It is in this respect that the distance is greatest between the High Schools and the schools bound by examinations in the school system. The Norwegian High Schools are more uniform as to structure, but like the Danish, they attach great importance to the boarding school form and the community spirit, which their environment encourages. The Swedish schools are marked by the division between the long winter courses, which often last 2 or 3 years, and a rapidly increasing number of courses, arranged parallel with the winter courses. The courses give recognized qualifications. The High Schools of Finland also have courses lasting 2–3 years. They are marked to some extent by the lines of study which give qualifications corresponding to what is given by the primary and lower secondary school and the upper secondary school. In addition, many of the High Schools have a purely business orientation.

Norway. For 400 years up to the Peace in Kiel in 1814, Norway was part of the Danish-Norwegian monarchy. Copenhagen was also Norway's capital. Danish was the written language. It is therefore not surprising that Norway was the first Nordic neighbouring country, where the Grundtvig educational ideas were widely accepted. In 1864, *Sagatun High School* at Hamar was founded by two of Grundtvig's disciples. In 1976 there were 88 High Schools. 39 were owned by Christian organisations. Nearly all the schools have a winter course of 33 weeks, beginning in August-September and ending in May-June. The schools have room for 160–190 boarders. Most of the teachers live in the schools. Emphasis is placed on work and leisure forming a whole.

The schools are not bound by fixed course programmes. Lines and subjects vary a great deal. At several schools, there are advanced courses for pupils with matriculation examination, and other advanced education. High Schools do not hold examinations, and do not give recognized qualifications, but when admitting students, some academic institutions also take it into consideration, if they have been through High School courses. The minimum age for High School pupils is 17 years at some schools, 18 at others.

Sweden. The first Swedish High School was started in 1868. In 1976 there were 108 High Schools in all. Differentiation is made between the county schools and the schools owned by the labour movement, the temperance movement, and Swedish Church and other private organisations. In the middle of the seventies, it was estimated that about half the High School pupils had their board and lodging at the schools. The rest are visitors, or live in private homes near the school. About 20% of the High Schools have branches (day High Schools) in the nearest large town.

In general, there is a 34-week winter course, which is built into the educational system with 2nd and 3rd year courses. However, there is a clear tendency away from this division of yearly courses in favour of grouping them in subjects and levels, and shorter courses. As a rule, there is a wide choice of subjects in the courses offered by the schools. The schools often specialize in international subjects, Third World problems, pre-paratory training in journalism, aesthetic subjects, and class instruction in theatre, drama and music at different levels, art and handicrafts. Music teachers are trained at some High Schools. Another form of professional training which is given at special courses of 2 years, is recreational teachers' training. But normally professional training is not provided at the High Schools.

The High School pupils stand on an equal footing as regards qualifications – obtained at year's courses and study courses –

with pupils possessing school leaving reports from primary schools, or a 2- or 3-year line at an upper secondary school, which gives admittance to advanced educational institutions and universities. The High Schools are not obliged to give reports or marks, but if a pupil wishes, he/she can obtain a statement on his/her suitability for advanced studies. – The minimum age for admittance to a High School is 18 years.

Finland, which Sweden ceded to Russia in 1809, was a Grand Duchy under the Russian Tsar up to its independence in 1917. In 1889, Sofia Hagman, who had personal experience of the Grundtvig High Schools, started the first Finnish-language High School, in *Kangsala*. The same year, the first Swedish-language High School was started in *Borgå*.

Out of Finland's 86 High Schools in 1975/76, 69 were Finnish-language, and 17 Swedish-language. The Folk High Schools usually have one-year courses, while the Folk Academies, which may be High School extensions or constitute independent units, generally have courses of 2 years' duration. Nearly all the schools have winter courses of at least 30 weeks, beginning in September and ending in May. The schools can also arrange short courses of at least 5 days. On the basis of the ideology they represent, one can group the High Schools in Grundtvigian (35 schools), Christian (36 schools) and schools run by a social or political organisation. They are all boarding schools. The laws give them great freedom in arranging their curricula. Most of them have lines preparing for examinations or a clearly professional aim, such as training of youth leaders.

The minimum age for admittance to a High School is 16 years before the end of the course. At Folk Academies, the minimum age is 17 years.

In the *Faroe Islands*, where the population constitutes a folk society with its own Home Rule within the Danish kingdom, two of Ernst Trier's former pupils started *The Faroes' Folk High School* in 1899. *Iceland*, which in 1944 cut the last State ties with Denmark and became an independent republic, obtained a Folk High School on the Danish model in 1972. This lies in Skálholt, with its cathedral and the old seat of the Bishop. In *Greenland*, which in 1953 became an integral part of the Danish kingdom and since 1979 has its own Home Rule, a High School was started in Holsteinsborg in 1962, *Knud Rasmussen's High School,* and *Sulissartut Højskoliat* in Qaqortoq (the Workers' High School in Julianehåb) in 1977.

Pupils can obtain State aid for a term at a High School in another Nordic country. If they are Danish, Norwegian, or Swedish citizens, they can receive the same allowances as for a High School term in their own country. For pupils from Finland, however, there are no such State allowances.

Countries other than the Nordic

In adult education without examinations, outside the North, it has generally proved to be difficult to introduce the boarding school form for courses over 3 months. But there are exceptions. In Great Britain, *Fircroft College* was started in Birmingham with Quaker support, *Coleg Harlech* in Wales, and *Newbattle Abbey* in Scotland – models of voluntary adult education. The founders of these schools had gathered inspiration during visits to Danish High Schools.

In Ireland, Dr. Noëlle Davies, who had been a pupil at the International High School in Helsingør, the clergyman Cormack Lloyd and his Danish-born wife, in co-operation with agricultural organisations, arranged cultural week-end courses on the lines of the Danish High School.

Holland also has a High School movement. There are prominent High School folk inspired by Grundtvig and Kold. Others have been to Swedish High Schools. The first Folk High School, in *Bakkeveen,* intended for young farmers, had 6-month courses, and the pupils were engaged in practical farming work for half the day. The pioneers, Dr. H. G. W. v.d. Vielen and Dr. H. D. de Vries regarded it as one of their tasks to build a bridge between Roman Catholics and Protestants, and to work against rootlessness among young people.

In Germany, after the First World War, organisations appeared, working for adult education, and these started the *Volkshochschulen,* which roughly corresponded to the Danish Evening High School. The *Heimvolkshochschulen*, which were more like the Danish Folk High Schools, were established chiefly in Northwest Germany. – Since 1949, the *Haus Sonnenberg* (Oberharz) has been a centre for conferences at international level, for international understanding. There has been considerable attendance from many countries at Sonnenberg's 10-day courses.

Poland received her first High School in 1924, started by Ignacy Solarz, who was familiar with the Danish Folk High Schools from visits to Denmark as a student. The Polish Folk High Schools were much occupied, from the start, with the peasants' struggle against social injustice. In 1944, the first Folk High School was started under the Communist regime, but after 1953, the political conditions forced many of the High Schools to close.

Adult education in Austria, which comes under the *Verbund der Volkshochschulen*, is related both to the Nordic Folk High Schools and the German Heimvolkshochschulen, and has good contacts with other countries. Religious and political questions, family questions and technical subjects particularly interest their pupils. The boarding school form, however, has only attracted a minority. Josef Steinberger (1874–1961), who took the first initiative, shared many of Grundtvig's ideas.

In Switzerland, a High School movement inspired by Grundtvig received an energetic champion in Fritz Wartenweiler. In 1910 he was a pupil at Ryslinge High School, later a teacher. He wrote a doctor's thesis on Grundtvig and founded the Folk High School *Frauenfeld*, where the 8-day courses were well attended. The *Verein der Volkshochschulen*, started in 1925, founded two Folk High Schools for young women. In 1935, the *Herzberg Volkshochschule* was started at Aarau, and here there has been an exchange of pupils with Danish High Schools.

With a view to letting Scandinavian High School folk get an idea of French rural culture, Professor Erica Simon arranged a cultural centre in an old farm, *Vanosc* near Lyons. After several study visits in Sweden and Denmark she felt that people in France could also learn something from the Nordic High Schools.

There are also instances where the Danish Grundtvig and Home Mission Folk High Schools have been transplanted overseas. Folk High Schools followed the wave of emigrants from Denmark to U.S.A., Canada and Argentina. In North America, the first was started in the Danish colony *Elk Horn*, Iowa, in 1878. In 1882 came *Ashland*, Michigan. In 1887 *Nysted Folk School* and a year later *Danebod* in Tyler, Minnesota. In 1911 *Atterdag College* in the Danish colony Solvang, California, and in 1921 *Dalum Folk School* in a Danish Colony in Canada. In Argentina a Danish High School was founded in *Cascallares*, in the province of Buenos Aires, on 5 June 1917 (The anniversary day of Denmark's Constitution).

None of these High Schools exist today. They had worked under great economic difficulties, as they did not have the same possibilities for State aid as the High Schools in Denmark. But for over 60 years they were visited by thousands of Danish immigrants and young people whose forefathers had cultural roots in Denmark.

XI.

THE HIGH SCHOOLS AND THE FUTURE

It will be of paramount importance, when faced with educational reforms which will bring the Danish system up to the level of the more elaborate systems of other countries, that the High Schools should be able to hold their own. It must never be forgotten that it is through the Folk High Schools that Denmark can make its contribution to international adult education, and that foreigners envy Denmark her special type of adult education. Nor has it been possible so far, outside Scandinavia, to raise funds, staffs, or students for such Folk High Schools on a large scale. The tradition is lacking. It was a lucky coincidence that gave us this tradition.

At the present moment, when a new school system is emerging, the Folk High Schools have every reason to safeguard their prestige. If, in the eyes of the general public, they should ever be reduced to some kind of substitute secondary school, their days would soon be numbered. And so in future, the High Schools must first of all concentrate on what makes them fundamentally different from all other types of schools.

In an era of mechanization and specialization, when much of what goes on after working hours becomes passive entertainment, served up by the television, or to the passive onlookers at some sports event, the High Schools are more greatly needed than ever, as a stimulant to individual energy and activity. And technical advances will hardly promote closer fellowship, in themselves. Together with the higher standard of living and increased leisure, they are more likely to produce isolation and rootlessness. That is, if things are allowed to slide.

When this rootlessness brings a sense of insecurity, when the cry for efficiency drives human beings along with their tongues hanging out of their mouths, from one examination to the next, when the demand for specialization splits the nation up into hundreds of small groups, each with its code language – in such an age there should be a forum where all social classes, all experts and specialists can meet and talk man to man. This is how we should visualize the future of the High Schools. We have need of a sanctuary where general education can flourish. Otherwise we shall have a specialist tyranny. To counteract this is one of the important tasks of the High Schools.

Then too, a High School course will always be an extra qualification for those applying for posts requiring a sympathetic understanding of other human beings, and a gift for co-operation. The community of the future will be based upon the individual's knack of doing his bit in a co-operative enterprise, so that he/she can both see it as a whole and make his/her own personal, critical appraisal. In this respect, the High Schools will be able to make their important contribution to trade and industry, the organizations, and political democracy – also in the future.

It will be possible to realise Grundtvig's conception in its original form, and not merely run schools for one social class. Today, with its friendly co-operation of teachers and students, the High School is more vividly alive than ever in the minds of the people. The individual will be enabled to deal with problems, the solution of which will help him to a clearer understanding of his responsibility to the community.

The High Schools, in spite of their wide range of variety, can serve as a link between the cultural life of our past and future. For they endeavour to enable every man and woman, each acording to his or her powers and interest, to share in our common cultural heritage, and at the same time to awaken in them a feeling of responsibility for the development of this heritage.

We, the teachers of the Danish Folk High Schools, have no doubt that they will be in still greater accord with the future than with the past. In the age of automation they will prove to be a leaven to humanity. They open the same prospects to the millions as to the *élite*. They bridge the cultural gulf.

Grundtvig's High School ideas are universal. In the future, too, there will be a need for High Schools which, in accord with Grundtvig's ideas, will be able to give our young people »heightened zest for life, greater maturity and self-confidence, and more understanding of human and civil living conditions«.

The Folk High Schools will continue to hold a key position in the Danish community.

XII.

LIST OF APPROVED FOLK HIGH SCHOOLS

(1 January 1980)

A guide to the nature and location of the Danish Folk High Schools affiliated to the Folk High School Secretariat (The Folk High School Information Office, Vartov, Farvergade 27, DK-1463 Copenhagen K., Tel. (01) 13 98 22) is given between the pages 32 and 33.

The *reference mark* * is used after some entries to indicate that enquiries should be made directly to the school.

Abbreviation: H.M. = School attached to the Home Mission in Denmark.

Andebølle Ungdomshøjskole
(Andebølle Youth High School, 1971)
DK-5492 Vissenbjerg, Funen

Ask højskole
(Ask High School, 1869)
DK-8340 Malling

Askov højskole
(Askov High School, 1865)
DK-6600 Vejen

Assens højskole
(Assens High School, 1978)
DK-5610 Assens

Bornholms Folkehøjskole
(Bornholm's Folk High School, 1867)
DK-3720 Aakirkeby

Borups højskole
(Borup's High School, 1891)
Frederiksholms Kanal 24
DK-1220 Copenhagen K.

Brandbjerg højskole ved Vejle
(Brandbjerg High School nr. Vejle, 1951)
DK-7300 Jelling

Brogården
(Brogården, Middelfart High School, 1964)
Strib, DK-5500 Middelfart

Børkop højskole
(Børkop High School, 1889) H. M.
Bible School
DK-7080 Børkop

Båring højskole
(Båring High School, 1959)
DK-5466 Asperup (nr. Middelfart)

Danebod højskole
(Danebod High School, 1920)
Fynshav, DK-6440 Augustenborg, Als

Den danske Husflidshøjskole
(The Danish Handicrafts High School, 1952)
DK-5300 Kerteminde

Den internationale Højskole
(The International High School, 1921)
DK-300 Helsingør

Den jyske Idrætsskole
(The Jutland Physical Training School, 1947)
DK-7100 Vejle

Den jyske Pensionisthøjskole
(The Jutland Pensioners High School, 1971)
Nørre Nissum, DK-7620 Lemvig

Den lille Højskole
(The Little High School, 1974)
Skjellerup, DK-9500 Hobro

Den rejsende Højskole *
(The Travelling High School, 1970)
Tvind, DK-6990 Ulfborg

Den rejsende Højskole i Juelsminde *
(The Travelling High School, 1978)
Kystvej, DK-7130 Juelsminde

Den rejsende Højskole i Vamdrup *
(The Travelling High School, 1979)
DK-6580 Vamdrup

Den røde højskole
(The Red High School, 1972)
Gerritsgade 56, DK-5700 Svendborg

Diakonhøjskolen *
(Nursing Sisters' High School, 1928)
DK-8270 Højbjerg

Egmont Højskolen
(Egmont High School, 1956)
Hou, DK-8300 Odder

Egå Ungdoms-Højskole
(Egå Youth High School, 1971)
Eghøjvej 31, DK-8250 Egå

Elbæk Folkehøjskole
(Elbæk Folk High School, 1979)
Elbæk, DK-8700 Horsens

Engelsholm højskole
(Engelsholm High School, 1940)
DK-7182 Bredsten v. Vejle

Esbjerg højskole
(Esbjerg (Workers) High School, 1910)
Stormgade 200, DK-6700 Esbjerg

Europahøjskolen
(Europe High School, 1976)
Ulvshale, DK-4780 Stege/Møn

Familiehøjskolen Skærgården
(Family High School Skærgården, 1972)
Skærbækvej 23, DK-7400 Herning

Forsknings-Højskolen
(Research High School, 1975)
Ribe Landevej 3,
DK-6100 Haderslev

Gerlev Idrætshøjskole
(Gerlev Physical Training High School, 1938)
DK-4200 Slagelse

Grundtvigs Højskole Frederiksborg
(Grundtvig's High School Frederiksborg, 1895)
Frederiksværksgade 147,
DK-3400 Hillerød

Gymnastikhøjskolen i Ollerup
(Gymnastics High School in Ollerup, 1920)
Svendborgvej 3,
DK-5762 Vester-Skerninge

Gymnastikhøjskolen ved Viborg
(Gymnastics High School at Viborg, 1951)
DK-8800 Viborg

Hadsten højskole
(Hadsten High School, 1877)
DK-8370 Hadsten

183

Haslev Højskole
(Haslev High School, 1891) H.M.
DK-4690 Haslev

Haslev udvidede Højskole
(Haslev Extended High School,
1920) H.M., YMCA & YWCA
DK-4690 Haslev

Herning højskole
(Herning High School, 1960)
Birk, DK-7400 Herning

Holstebro Højskole
(Holstebro High School, 1973)
Nørregade 44, DK-7500 Holstebro

Hoptrup Højskole
(Hoptrup High School, 1920) H.M.,
YMCA & YWCA
DK-6100 Haderslev

Idrætshøjskolen i Sønderborg
(Physical Training High School in
Sønderborg, 1952)
DK-6400 Sønderborg

Idrætshøjskolen i Århus
(Physical Training High School in
Århus, 1971)
Vejlby Centervej, DK-8240 Risskov

*International Apostolsk Højskole i
Kolding*
(International Apostolic High
School in Kolding, 1950)
Lykkegårdsvej 100,
DK-6000 Kolding

Jaruplund Højskole Sydslesvig
(Jaruplund High School South
Slesvig, 1950)
D-2391 Jaruplund-Weding/BRD

Knud Rasmussens højskole
(Knud Rasmussen's High School,
1962)
Box 82, DK-3911 Holsteinsborg,
Greenland

Kolding Højskole
(Kolding High School, 1972)
Skovvangen 18, DK-6000 Kolding

Kolt Ældrehøjskole
(Kolt High School for Senior
Citizens, 1971)
Beringsvej 1, DK-8361 Hasselager J.

Krabbesholm højskole
(Krabbesholm High School, 1907)
DK-7800 Skive

Krogerup højskole
(Krogerup High School, 1940)
DK-3050 Humlebæk

Kunsthøjskolen
(Art High School, 1965)
DK-4300 Holbæk

Kvindehøjskolen (Den nordiske)
(Women's High School, The Nordic,
1979)
Visby, DK-6270 Tønder

*Køng Folkehøjskole
Den vestfynske idrætshøjskole*
(Køng Folk High School, The West
Funen Physical Training
High School, 1877)
DK-5620 Glamsbjerg

Lollands højskole
(Lolland's High School, 1905)
Højskolevej 79, DK-4920 Søllested

LO-skolen
(LO (Trade Unions) School, 1969)
DK-3000 Helsingør

Luthersk Missionsforenings Højskole
(Lutheran Mission Union's High
School, 1923)
Fredensborgvej 9,
DK-3400 Hillerød

Løgumkloster Højskole
(Løgumkloster High School, 1960)
DK-6240 Løgumkloster

Marielyst Pensionisthøjskole *
(Marielyst Pensioners High School,
1971)
DK-4873 Væggerløse

Nordiska folkhögskolan i Kungälv
(Nordic Folk High School in
Kungälv, 1947)
S-442 25 Kungälv, Sweden

Nørgaards Højskole, Gudenaadalen
(Nørgaard's High School
Gudenaadalen, 1955)
Vestre Ringvej 9,
DK-8850 Bjerringbro

Nørre Nissum højskole og efterskole
(Nørre Nissum High School
and Continuation School,
1887) H.M.
DK-7620 Lemvig

Odder højskole
(Odder High School, 1889)
DK-8300 Odder

Pensionisthøjskolen Rude Strand
(Pensioners High School Rude
Strand, 1973)
Kystvejen 114, DK-8300 Odder

Pinsevækkelsens højskole
(Pentecostal Movement High
School, 1956)
DK-9550 Mariager

Roskilde højskole
(Roskilde High School, 1907)
DK-4000 Roskilde

Ry højskole
(Ry High School, 1892)
DK-8680 Ry

Ryslinge højskole, Fyn
(Ryslinge High School, Funen,
1867)
DK-5856 Ryslinge

Rødding Højskole
(Rødding High School, 1844)
DK-6630 Rødding, South Jutland

Rødkilde højskole
(Rødkilde High School, 1865)
DK-4780 Stege

Rønde højskole
(Rønde High School, 1897) H.M.
DK-8410 Rønde

Rønshoved højskole
(Rønshoved High School, 1921)
DK-6340 Kruså

Silkeborg Højskole
(Silkeborg High School, 1969)
DK-8600 Silkeborg

Skælskør Folkehøjskole
(Skælskør Folk High School, 1908)
(Antvorskov High School)
DK-4230 Skælskør

Snoghøj nordisk folkehøjskole
(Snoghøj Nordic Folk High School,
1913)
DK-7000 Fredericia

Højskolen Solhavegården
(Solhavegården High School, 1979)
DK-3060 Espergærde (nr.
Helsingør)

Sproghøjskolen på Kalø
(Language High School on Kalø,
1952)
DK-8410 Rønde

Store Restrup højskole
(Store Restrup High School, 1965)
DK-9240 Nibe

Støvring højskole
(Støvring High School, 1897)
DK-9530 Støvring, Himmerland

Sulissartut Højskoliat *
(Workers' High School in
Julianehåb, 1977)
Postbox 132, DK-3920 Qaqortoq,
Greenland

Søhus Gartnerhøjskole
(Søhus Horticultural High School,
1975)
Slettensvej 216, DK-5270 Odense N.

Testrup højskole
(Testrup High School, 1865)
DK-8320 Maarslet

Tidens Højskole
(High School of the Day, 1973)
Isterød, DK-2970 Hørsholm

Tølløse højskole
(Tølløse High School, 1909)
DK-4340 Tølløse

Ubberup Højskole
(Ubberup High School, 1899)
DK-4400 Kalundborg

Uge Folkehøjskole
(Uge Folk High School, the Nordic
Folk High School in South Jutland,
1977)
DK-6360 Tinglev

Uldum højskole
(Uldum High School, 1848)
DK-7171 Uldum

Ungdomshøjskolen ved Ribe
(Youth High School at Ribe, 1971)
V. Vedsted, DK-6760 Ribe

Unge Hjems højskole
(Young Homes High School, 1960)
DK-8270 Højbjerg

Vallekilde højskole
(Vallekilde High School, 1865)
DK-4534 Hørve

Vestbirk højskole
(Vestbirk High School, 1884)
DK-8752 Østbirk

Vestjyllands højskole
(West Jutland's High School, 1969)
DK-6950 Ringkøbing

Vrå folkehøjskole
(Vrå Folk High School, 1872)
DK-9760 Vrå

Ærø Folkehøjskole
(Ærø Folk High School, 1978)
DK-5970 Ærøskøbing

XIII.

BIBLIOGRAPHY

Adult education in the Nordic countries. Published by the Nordic Council and the Secretariat for Nordic Cultural Cooperation. 1976.

Allcock, J. G. M. (ed.): *School Systems – A Guide.* Council of Europe, Strassbourg.

Begtrup, H., Lund, H. and Manniche, P.: *The Folk High Schools of Denmark and the Development of a Farming Community.* O. U. P. London, 1948.

Campbell, Olive Dame: *The Danish Folk High School.* Macmillan. New York. 1928.

Canfield, A. T.: *Folk High Schools in Denmark and Sweden: A comparative analysis.* Comparative Education Review. 1965.

Davies, Noëlle: *Educational Life.* Williams and Norgate. London. 1931.

Davis, D. C.: *The Danish Folk High School:* An experiment in humanistic education. University Microfilms Ltd., Ann Arbor, Michigan. 1970.

Dixon, W.: *Education in Denmark.* Harrop, London. 1958.

Dixon, W.: *Society Schools and Progress in Scandinavia.* Pergamon. Oxford. 1965.

Engberg, Poul: *The Scandinavian Folk High Schools.* Odense. 1963.

Fleure, H. J.: *The Path to International Understanding.* Adult Education in the struggle for peace. Edited by Peter Manniche. Gad. Copenhagen. 1949.

Grundtvig, N. F. S.: *Selected Writings.* Ed. by Johannes Knudsen. Philadelphia, Pa. Fortress Pr. 1976.

Hart, Joseph K.: *Light from the North.* H. Holt & Co., New York. 1926.

King, E. R.: *Other Schools and Ours.* Holt, Rinehart and Winston. New York. 1973.

Knudsen, Johannes: *Danish Rebel.* A study of N. F. S. Grundtvig. Muhlenberg Press, Philadelphia. 1955.

Lund, Ragnar: *Scandinavian Adult Education.* Copenhagen. 1952.

Manniche, Peter: *Rural development in Denmark and the changing countries of the world.* Borgen. Copenhagen. 1978.

Mortensen, Enok: *Schools for Life.* Danish American Heritage Society. Solvang. California. 1977.

Nellemann, Aksel: *Schools and Education in Denmark.* Det danske Selskab, Copenhagen. 1972.

Nielsen, Ernst D.: *N. F. S. Grundtvig.* An American study. Angustan Press. Rock Island, Illinois. 1955.

Paulston, Rolland G.: *Other Dreams other Schools: Folk Colleges in Social and Ethnic Movements*. University Center for International Studies, Univ. of Pittsburgh. 1980.

Rasmussen, V.: *Birth of a new Folk High School*. Danish Journal. Ministry of Foreign Affairs. Copenhagen. 1972.

Skrubbeltrang, F.: *The Danish Folk High School*. Det danske Selskab, Copenhagen. 1953.

Thaning, K.: *N. F. S. Grundtvig*. Det danske Selskab, Copenhagen. 1972.

Thrane, E.: *Education and Culture in Denmark*. Gad. Copenhagen. 1958.

Thut, J. N. and Adams, D.: *Education Patterns in Contemporary Societies*. Mac Graw Hill. New York. 1964.

XIV.

INDEX

The letters *æ*, *ø*, *å* (in that order) follow z in the Danish alphabet and entries containing these special Danish vowel signs are alphabetized accordingly; *aa* is identical with *å*.

189

What can we learn from one another?

Aim and work of the Danish Institute

Det danske Selskab, The Danish Institute is an independent nonprofit institution for cultural exchange between Denmark and other countries. Abroad its aims is to inform other countries about life and culture in Denmark, particularly in the field of education, welfare services and other branches of sociology; at home to help spread knowledge of cultural affairs in other countries. Its work of information is thus based on the idea of mutuality and treated as a comparative study of cultural development at home and abroad by raising the question: What can we learn from one another? The work of the Danish Institute is done mainly in three ways:

1) By branches of the Danish Institute abroad – in Great Britain (Edinburgh), the Benelux countries (Brussels), France (Rouen), Switzerland (Zürich), Italy (Milan), West Germany (Dortmund) and its contacts in the USA and other countries. Lectures, reference work, the teaching of Danish, exhibitions, concerts, film shows, radio and television programmes as well as study tours and summer schools are an important part of the work of representatives of the Institutes that have been established abroad.

2) Summer seminars and study tours both in Denmark and abroad. Participants come from Denmark and other countries. The study tours bring foreign experts to Denmark and take Danish experts abroad. Teachers, librarians, architects and persons engaged in social welfare and local government make up a large part.

3) Publication of books and reference papers in foreign languages. Primary and Folk High Schools in Denmark, the library system, welfare services, cooperative movement, handicrafts, architecture, literature, art and music, life and work of prominent Danes are among the main subjects.

The author Martin A. Hansen called the Danish Institute a Folk High School beyond the borders: »In fact the work of the Danish Institute abroad has its roots in our finest traditions of popular education, which go right back to Grundtvig and Kold. The means and methods used are modern, the materials the very best and the approach to the work is cultural in the truest meaning of the word.«

DET DANSKE SELSKAB

The Danish Institute for Information about Denmark and Cultural Cooperation with other Nations

KULTORVET 2, DK-1175 COPENHAGEN, DENMARK

Publications in English:

DANISH INFORMATION HANDBOOKS

Schools and Education – The Danish Folk High Schools – Special Education in Denmark – Public Libraries in Denmark – Social Welfare in Denmark – Local Government in Denmark – The Danish Cooperative Movement

DENMARK IN PRINT AND PICTURES

The Danish Church – Danish Architecture – Danish Painting and Sculpture – Danish Design – Industrial Life in Denmark – The Story of Danish Film – Sport in Denmark – Garden Colonies in Denmark – Copenhagen, Capital of a Democracy – Aarhus, Meeting Place of Tradition and Progress – The Limfjord, its Towns and People – Funen, the Heart of Denmark

In preparation:

Women in Denmark

DANES OF THE PRESENT AND PAST

Danish Literature – Contemporary Danish Composers – Arne Jacobsen, by P. E. Skriver – Søren Kierkegaard, by Frithiof Brandt – N. F. S. Grundtvig, by Kaj Thaning

DANISH REFERENCE PAPERS

The Danish Mother's Aid Centres – Employers and Workers – The Ombudsman – Care of the Aged in Denmark

PERIODICALS

Contact with Denmark. Published annually in English, French, German, Italian, Netherlandish.
Musical Denmark, nos. 1–30. Published annually in English.